THE BEAST

To Kathy:

A. Mathers

THE BEAST

Scott Mathews

NEW DEGREE PRESS
COPYRIGHT © 2021 SCOTT MATHEWS
All rights reserved.

THE BEAST

ISBN
978-1-63730-831-8 *Paperback*
978-1-63730-893-6 *Kindle Ebook*
978-1-63730-957-5 *Digital Ebook*

To everyone who believed in me when I couldn't.

CONTENTS

AUTHOR'S NOTE	9
PROLOGUE	13
ONE	29
TWO	41
THREE	49
FOUR	59
FIVE	71
SIX	79
SEVEN	95
EIGHT	115
NINE	133
TEN	149
ELEVEN	169
TWELVE	183
THIRTEEN	191
FOURTEEN	209
FIFTEEN	225
NOTES	233
ACKNOWLEDGMENTS	235

AUTHOR'S NOTE

Where were you when you realized your life wasn't what you wanted it to be? Lying in bed, staring up at the ceiling? Or sitting on your couch, scrolling through photos of people on vacations in beautiful places, surrounded by loved ones? Maybe you weren't home at all; you were at a bar, a park, a beach, or a bowling alley when you felt a strange, gentle tap on the shoulder. You'd turn around and find Dread two inches from your nose.

    I was in my car. I'd had a huge falling out with a loved one about a week prior, and I was an absolute mess. Couldn't eat or sleep, couldn't even watch TV because the shows I liked became shows *we* liked, which mutated into sad, unbearable taunts. It was like going through withdrawal. Every moment of those first few days was fixated on her. She completed me; she made me whole. She was the scaffolding supporting the crumbling bridge of my distressed, ill brain. She held me up for years, both during and after college. I relied on her because I never thought we'd part ways, so I did what every beer-soaked college student does: I forgot. The bridge held; my work got better, my life improved, and I was happy. But I forgot how big the holes in me she was filling were. And then she was gone, and the bridge collapsed.

It doesn't take much to conjure up Dread. A familiar song at the wrong moment, a comforting scent, or even something as small as a single word can make its insidious presence known. On that particular morning, sitting in my car, I was feeling okay. Better than I had been, anyway. I had survived the first week of work after the split. Life felt livable again; the bridge was slowly being rebuilt. If life were a movie, this is where I'd freeze in a pained but determined tableau as the screen faded to black and the credits rolled. Everything sorted and squared. But this isn't a movie, and nothing so big is ever truly sorted or squared. I looked out the window and saw the car she used to drive parked across the street.

When I was very young and terrified of everything, my dad used to lay with me in bed when I was overwhelmed. He'd tell me that life is just a big roller coaster, full of ups and downs, but ultimately a fun, fulfilling experience. Now that I'm older, I can look back over my life and realize he was only about half-right. Life is, in fact, a roller coaster, but it is by no means fun nor fulfilling. Julijonas Urbonas designed an art piece called the *Euthanasia Coaster*, an enormous roller coaster with one incredibly high drop that rockets a car full of passengers into several consecutive loops which progressively tighten. These loops generate enough force to push all the blood out of the passengers' brains for so long, they die.[1] That's life. The whole, messy thing. The hopeful ascent of childhood, the sheer drop of adolescence, and the death spiral of adulthood.

Now that the more existentially fearful readers are hyperventilating, let me finish my first story. Seeing that black Mazda ravaged all semblance of progress I'd made over that first agonizing week of self-reliance. I thought the bridge had collapsed, and I'd have to start all over again, but it didn't. Not completely, anyway. Sure, there were still huge holes and weak points that would need to be re-rebuilt, but some of the fresh bricks and beams held. In that moment, I realized even if the repairs took a lifetime to complete, at least they could be completed. Trying to take comfort in that felt impossible at the time because climbing out of the misery hole is like trying to walk down a bowling lane without faceplanting. Still, as the weeks marched unstoppably on, it got easier. I started reaching out to old friends again, discovering new hobbies, doing whatever I could to fill the maddeningly quiet hours of a pandemic day. Silly things my housemates did became less irritating and funnier. I surrounded myself with people who complemented me, not completed me.

Slowly, the bridge came together, brick by brick, beam by beam, until it stood tall and whole and strong again. I knew there would be more impossible days ahead, days when I wouldn't be able to do anything but fixate on the stubborn cracks in the bridge and wait for Dread to come seeping out like pus, but I also knew those days couldn't last forever. One day those cracks wouldn't be ugly marks of weakness or failure but unique blemishes of history I could look at to remember how much I'd built for myself.

This book is for anyone who feels like they can't peel themselves away from the cracks in their own bridges. I know the feeling. I know what it is to stare up at the sky from deep inside the misery hole, desperately wishing and pleading for a way out. It felt—and sometimes continues to feel—impossible. But I promise it isn't. Dread has a funny way of destroying things, turning happy memories and thoughts into wrecking balls and explosives. I've watched everything collapse, and it was horrible beyond words. But nothing destroyed cannot be rebuilt, and it was worth every moment of struggle.

This story is deeply personal to me. It explores several scenarios similar to my own experiences. The inescapable despair and the hopeful longing for connection are reminiscent of real feelings and thoughts the people around me and I have wrangled with. While the characters and actions may be simply fiction, the emotions and discoveries our characters explore are anything but fictional. It's never too late to start rebuilding your bridge.

PROLOGUE

Congratulations, Graduates! reads the banner hung over the doors into the dining hall in cheap, cloying colors. I'd have thought someone would've taken them down after December graduation, but now that it's the end of April, they might as well leave it up for the May graduates too. The noise in the serving area is unbearable, or maybe that's just my hangover. The serving area bustles with students filling meal boxes with eggs, toast, sausage, waffles, and all manner of last-minute breakfast fixings while they chat about summer plans, job opportunities, or something equally as bland. Everyone's talking so loud, trying to be heard over the din of everyone else talking so loud. It's a vicious cycle with head-splitting consequences.

Devon Hill, my roommate, makes his way back to me and snatches one of the sausage links out of my box. He and I have been living together since freshman year. Who would've guessed my random roommate assignment would be my common-law spouse? I act like I don't notice; I did take the last eight, after all. This might be the last University breakfast run, so I really need to make it count. His box is full to the brim with pancakes, syrup practically pouring out the top. The thought of all that sugar makes my stomach turn.

"You should get some eggs," I tell him. "They'll replenish the enzymes your liver's used up. It'll help with your hangover."

"Where'd you learn that?" He looks down at his pancakes, trying to spot some room where eggs could go.

"Read it somewhere."

That's code for "I watched a video from a sketchy medical channel on YouTube."

"Neat, but eggs make me gag. So..." He turns on his heels and wanders off to the drink cooler.

"Grab me a Gatorade!"

Gatorade always hits the spot whenever I'm hungover, especially the light purple flavor. Oh, yeah, that one always does it for me. That crisp, sorta grape, sorta synthetic flavor cuts right through all of the stale booze and morning breath. Thinking about it makes me realize how dry my mouth is. I work my tongue against the roof of my mouth as I get in the long checkout line. Devon better get back before I pay, because once I sit down, I will not be getting back up.

Two girls in front of me start to cackle, making my head throb. The redhead is holding her phone up for the one with glasses to see. Looking between the two of them, I see a picture that makes my stomach sour. Some dude, slumped over in a bathtub, completely passed out and covered in puke. In the corner of the frame, there's a little metal toilet paper stand laying on a green bath mat next to the tub. I definitely recognize that bathroom from the frat party Devon and I went to last night. Looks like somebody had a little too much fun. I suddenly feel way too hot as my stomach coils up like an angry snake.

I could really use that Gatorade.

The glasses girl covers her mouth with a hand to stifle her raucous laughter. It doesn't work nearly as well as she thinks it does. "Did you take that yourself?"

"And all of these." The redhead nods and swipes on her phone.

I only see two more pictures, each from a different angle, before I shut my eyes. Their horrible laughter coupled with the mental picture of all that puke is making me unsteady.

"Doing all right there, bud?" Devon puts a hand on my shoulder. I open my eyes to see him offering me a bottle. I snatch it up and rip the cap off. Half the bottle is gone before it comes away from my lips. "I guess Powerade works too."

"Much better now." The ice-cold drink swirls in my stomach, cooling and calming my unhappy guts. Electrolytes set to reviving my withering cells while the sugar gives me a much-needed kick. I still don't feel good, but I do feel better.

I pay for our meals, and we make our way over to a small, square table near the back of the dining hall. It is not exactly ideal since the entire back wall is floor-to-ceiling windows that let in too much sunlight, but it beats sitting with random strangers. I can't handle that much stimulation right now. I think my head would pop.

We sit, Devon diving head-first into his pancakes. The man is a human garbage disposal, wolfing down pancakes like he hasn't eaten in a month. Syrup dribbles down his chin as I tease at my food with a fork, my appetite quickly vanishing.

"Could you maybe slow down there?" I finally ask him. "Nobody's gonna take it away from you, and you're making me nauseous."

Devon laughs and wipes his mouth on a napkin. "Sorry! I'm starving. A hard night of drinking always builds a big appetite. For me, anyway."

I push a forkful of eggs and sausage into my mouth and slowly chew. I know I need to swallow, but I also don't want to upset my stomach any more than I already have. I gulp it down, hoping it settles.

"Yeah. Speak for yourself."

I continue picking at my food while Devon dives back into his meal. He's a fucking animal, but his ability to consume anything always comes in handy when we have leftovers I don't want.

"What'd you wanna do today?" he asks through a mouthful of pancake.

I force myself to swallow my third bite of food before answering. "Something low-key. I am in no state for doing anything crazy." I spear more breakfast on my fork but leave it sitting upright in the box.

"We could go see a movie. I think that new *Saw* flick's out now."

"They're still making *Saw* movies? Which one are they on now? Twelve?"

Devon sits back and laughs his deep, ringing laugh. A few annoyed, likely hungover, students look over at the noise and grimace.

"Think you'd be up for it?" He scrapes the syrup off the fork into his mouth with his lips, then points it at me. "Then we can just hang at home tonight. Let you dry out a little."

I chuckle and shake my head. "I really don't know how you do it."

"It just takes practice. You'll get there." He pulls his phone out and unlocks it. "You check movie times. I'll check Uber prices."

Before I can fish my phone out, it goes off, buzzing wildly against my leg. I pull it out and check the screen before shooting Devon a sheepish look. "Mind if I take this?"

He furrows his mouth to one side and sucks air in over his teeth. "It's Amelia, isn't it?"

I give him a little nod.

"Ah!" He drapes his hand across his face like a damsel in distress. "Young love comes to steal you away from me again!"

I roll my eyes and flip him off, which only makes him laugh. "I need to stop telling you shit when I drink." I stand up from the table and make my way out of the building.

Last night, I drunkenly told Devon I'm wildly in love with our friend, Amelia. We'd all met at the end of sophomore year. We were buying a couch from her because Devon and I were moving off campus into a little duplex and needed some cheap furniture. She and Devon got along fine, but she and I hit it off right away, probably because we're both sarcastic assholes. While Devon was measuring the couch, Amelia and I chatted about summer plans. Turned out we were both staying at school that summer to hammer out some prerequisites, so she gave me her number to keep in touch. Less than two weeks later, we were hooking up. We decided to keep things casual, but I knew we had this unspoken agreement our relationship would get more serious in the future. We have stayed friends ever since.

I plop down on a bench outside and answer my phone. "Hey, you. What's up?"

"What're you doing right now?" Amelia's voice is bright and melodic as she speeds through her question.

"Well, I was getting breakfast with Devon, and we—"

"Was, as in you're done now, right?" She's bristling with energy. Normally, I love that about her, but right now, it's making me want to bore a hole in my skull.

"Why are you asking?"

"Do you wanna come on a hike with me?"

Oh, Jesus.

"It's the first nice day since, like, last year, and I wanna do something outside!" Amelia is always dragging me out on last-minute adventures. She's got a grudge against making plans, I swear.

"Hold on, hold on." I look over my shoulder to make sure Devon hasn't come out of the dining hall yet. "It's supposed to be nice tomorrow too. Could we do something then?"

"Can't tomorrow. Busy. That's why we should go today!" She's always busy when I'm free. Plus hiking? Right now? I'm pretty sure I'd just keel over and die after the first ten minutes. But it is more time to spend with her.

I'm definitely gonna need more Powerade.

"All right, fine. When did you wanna go?"

"Where are you? I can pick you up now, and we—"

"You wanna go *now*?"

Is she trying to kill me?

I wipe at the sweat beading on my forehead from the strenuous activity of standing upright outside. "I'd need to talk to Devon before I—"

"Talk to Devon about what?" Devon says behind me, making me drop my phone and jump out of my skin.

"What have I said about sneaking up on me?" I bite.

"That it's both easy and fun to do." He smirks, clearly pleased with himself. "What's going on?"

I pick my phone up and press it back to my ear. "Still there?"

"Yeah, I'm here. You all right over there? Sounded like you fell down some stairs or something."

"I'm fine. Gimme two seconds." I shoot Devon a look and pull the phone away from my ear, muting it. "Amelia's asking if I can go hiking with her right now, and I said I needed to ask you first because we just made plans."

"I see. Well, do you wanna go?"

I make a face at him. "No. I'm just trying to be difficult."

"Oh, perfect!" He chuckles, cracking a smile. "If you wanna go, then go."

That was surprisingly easy.

"Are you sure?"

"Yeah. There are movie times all day, so maybe we can catch it in the evening or something."

"Sounds good to me. I'll catch you later then."

Devon starts walking back to our house off-campus. Taking myself off mute, I put the phone back to my ear.

"Alright, Amelia. I'm up for a hike."

My arms strain as I struggle to pull my chest over the ledge's lip. I try swinging my leg up, but I can't get it over.

This is what I get for wearing tight pants and making last-minute plans.

I let my leg drop and lower myself to the ground. Taking a few steps back, I suck in a quick breath.

A little more momentum wouldn't hurt.

I run up and grab the edge, using the speed to propel my leg up. But the tip of my shoe catches the edge rather than going over it. I lose my grip and, suddenly, I'm on my ass. She said this would be an easy hike on the drive over. I think she lied.

"Need a hand down there?"

I look up at Amelia, shit-eating grin plastered across her face. I see myself stand up and dust off in her mirrored sunglasses.

"Oh, no, I'm doing just fine, thanks," I call back up to her. "I'm having a blast."

"You're the one who wanted to wear skinny jeans."

"You're the one who wouldn't let me stop home and change!" I wipe my forehead with the hem of my shirt. I don't think I've ever been this damp outside of a pool. Dad always used to tell me that we Paulsens never pass out from the heat because we sweat so much. At this point, I'm less worried about the heat and more worried about drowning. "And this is more like a climb than a hike if you ask me."

"You should'a worn shorts like I told ya," she says in a singsong voice. She's enjoying my frustration, and I'm more than happy to play it up for her enjoyment.

"Oh, right! The shorts I definitely have because we definitely stopped at my house so I could change! Gosh, Amelia, you're so right."

"Glad you're seeing things my way." She sits on the ledge and kicks her legs back and forth in amusement. I shake my head and step back for another running start. She drives me crazy in all the right ways.

I hit the dirt wall hard but hold tight. My leg swings up... before the dirt I'm holding onto comes loose, and I bust ass again.

"God damnit!" I slap at the ground, trying to vent my building frustration, but only feeling childish.

"Still having a blast there, Butthead?" she sputters between laughs. She's called me Butthead for as long as I've known her. Her version of a pet name. "Need a hand?"

"Yes, Amelia, I clearly need a hand."

She smiles and stands up, stretching her arms tall over her head. Her elbow pops loudly, making me wince. She brings her arms back down, pressing the back of her hands into her hips like an angry parent might. "Not if you're gonna be nasty."

This is a lot less funny when I'm the one on the butt end of it.

"Will you just fuckin' help me, please?" As much as I enjoy our little verbal spars, they have a nasty habit of feeling much meaner than Amelia intends.

"Fine, fine, fine." Amelia pulls out her hair tie, letting her long brown hair unspool with a shake of her head. She collects it all back up, smoothing down any stray, wild strands, and puts it in a fresh ponytail. "Gimme your hand."

She crouches down and leans out. I extend my left hand up to her and grab the ledge with my right.

"Try not to rip my arm off." The last thing I need is a dislocated shoulder, and she's much stronger than she looks.

Her pulling is just enough for my foot to find purchase on the edge. She pushes up from crouched to standing as I get my back knee up over the ledge. With one last tug, I'm standing. I drop my head and lean forward, putting my hands on my knees to catch my breath.

"See?" Amelia pats her hands on her shorts, wiping away my palm sweat. "Not so bad."

I turn my head up to say something snarky, but she's turned around to scope out the trail. She's wearing a tie-dye tank top and jean shorts that make her ass look amazing. She's rooting around in a light gray, L.L. Bean backpack for something I can't see. Her skin glints in the flecks of sunlight finding its way through the canopy above.

"Stop staring at my ass." She looks over her shoulder at me and smiles.

"Can you read minds or something?" I push off my knees to stand upright.

"Just yours." She sets her backpack on the ground and tosses a water bottle at me. I catch it to my chest. "You should hydrate after all that *exercise*." She pulls her own water bottle out of the bag and takes a long sip.

"Who tells you you're funny?" I open the bottle and drink. I actually am super thirsty.

She's always got just the thing.

"Don't finish it all!"

The sudden urgency in her voice makes me pull the quickly-emptying bottle away from my mouth.

"Why?"

"We might need some to wash the dirt off your face after you eat shit on the next climb."

I roll my eyes and cap the bottle. "All right, all right, enough of that." I toss the bottle back to her. "Stick that back in there, would you?"

"It's weird hearing you say that when the sun's up." She winks as my face reddens and screws up in mock disgust.

"Just put the bottle away, you nasty beasty, you."

She blows me a kiss and drops it in the bag before slinging it back over her shoulder. "Speaking of nasty beasties, how much does Devon know about us?"

That's a dangerous question. "More than you" would definitely be a bad answer.

"Where's that coming from?"

Amelia adjusts the straps on her bag, keeping her eyes off me. "Well, this isn't the first time you've canceled plans with him to hang out with me, and I'm just curious if it bothers him."

I turn away from her and stare out past the trail.
How the hell am I supposed to know if it bothers him?
"No, it doesn't bother him. Why would it? I mean, he's—well, you know. Eh, maybe not, but he's—it's fine, he gets it. We're just—well, you know...." The words dribble out in chunky globs like spoiled milk.

Amelia's hand on my shoulder stops my babbling. "Easy there, my dude." Her arm slides across my back as she steps behind me, her other hand coming up to rest on my chest. "It's not that big a deal."

I take a deep breath, feeling more comfortable with her surrounding me. A sheepish smile creeps across my face.

"You always know how to fluster me." My hand comes up to meet hers on my shoulder.

"It's a gift." She pats my chest and pulls away. "Come on, we shouldn't be too far now. You're gonna love this." She turns and continues up the trail. I give one last look out before following her forward.

Aside from the climbs, the trail hasn't been all that steep. A little uphill, for sure, but nothing unreasonable. And then we reach the final push. *Sweet baby Jesus, I'm earning my mountain goat stripes today for not sliding straight back down the mountain.*

Amelia has no issue, finding good traction on every step in her boots. My running shoes, however, aren't holding up so well. Thankfully, the trees have plenty of low-hanging branches I can grab if I slip... again. I'm quickly losing steam while Amelia trucks on ahead. She's clearly already got those mountain goat stripes because she's killing it while I'm—well, being killed. My headache's come back with a vengeance. Whether it's a hangover aftershock or just dehydration is anyone's guess, but I am officially struggling.

After another couple of minutes, my body is in full meltdown mode. I'm huffing and puffing, desperately trying to keep my lungs from catching fire, and my legs are screaming for a break. My sweating has only gotten worse. The salt and bug spray keep dripping into my eyes, so I'm pretty much blind at this point too. This hike has easily been the most strenuous thing I've done in months.

I'm gonna be sore for a few days after this. But being with Amelia makes it worthwhile.

"Jared!" she calls from up ahead.

"I'm comin'!" I gasp between breaths. "I'm comin'." I wipe my forehead with my equally wet hand, succeeding only in making myself feel even grosser. She's gotten far enough ahead that I can't see her.

Mercifully, the trail levels off as I break through the trees into a clearing. A few shrubs and saplings are scattered around, but the dirt trail has given way to huge swaths of buried stone, leaving little room for large foliage to grow.

"Come here!" Amelia motions to me. She's sitting on a huge flat rock, with her legs crossed and her bag on her lap. I shakily climb up and sit behind her, extending my legs alongside hers. She leans back into my chest. "Isn't it gorgeous?"

I take her sunglasses off her head and rest my chin there, looking out over the forest below. The rock we're sitting on rests on the cusp of what has to be a sheer hundred-foot fall. I can see everything from here. Miles and miles of trees, so small they look like painted miniatures. No power lines or roads, just trees of all different sizes and shapes, clustered together, forming the verdant canopy below. The afternoon sun is just beginning to set, the cerulean sky showing the slightest traces of orange and pink.

"If you look over there—" She points over to the right. "Can you see the break in the trees? Where the river runs through? If you listen closely, you can just barely hear it."

I wrap my arms around her chest, feeling her heart beat on top of mine as we both listen for the burbling.

About when I think I can hear it, my phone goes off, completely overpowering the sound. I pull it out.

Howdy, partner. What's up? Devon's text reads.

Amelia rolls her head back to look up at me. "Who's that?"

"Just Devon," I tell her.

She rolls her eyes. "Tell your husband I say hi."

I bop her on the forehead and give her the "be nice" look as another message comes through.

The last movie time for tonight's around eight-ish, and I think it's about four-thirty, five-ish now. Should I pick up the tickets?

I look at Amelia, her brown eyes sparkling in the sunlight.

I'm not sure, I send back.

I'm not ready for this moment to end.

How about I just text you or something when we leave, okay? Sounds good. Just stop by my room and say hi when you get in.

Will do, mate! I send off and tuck my phone back into my pocket.

"How's your husband?" Amelia puts her head forward, looking back out over the cliff.

"Devon and I have only lived together for four years, which you know. Four years is not enough time to constitute common-law marriage anywhere."

"Oh, I'm so *sorry*." She clutches at invisible pearls around her neck.

"And, to answer your question, he's fine, I guess. I dunno. He's hard to read sometimes. Keeps a lot of that shit close to his belt, y'know?"

"Fair enough." She rummages around in her bag, producing a pack of cigarettes and a lighter. "Want one?"

"If you're offering."

She lights one, giving it a few puffs before handing it off to me and lighting her own. Little wisps of smoke curl in the breeze as we stare out silently.

She has to feel it too. She has to. I should just ask her right now. But if I'm wrong, this whole thing goes to shit. Two years down the drain. I don't want to ruin this by wanting more.

I trace little circles on her forearm with my fingers. She feels so familiar pressed against me like this, like she's a part of me. Whether it's in bed or on top of a mountain, this feels like where we're supposed to be. It's so real and so, so terrifying. I take a long drag on my smoke, trying to decide what to do.

I've still got time. Graduation isn't for—what? Two, three weeks? I shouldn't rush this. If I've got time, might as well use it. Make sure this won't blow up in my face.

"Are you looking forward to your program thing after graduation?" I ask her.

She blows two lines of smoke from her slender nose. "I'm actually meeting up with a guy from the conservatory tomorrow."

"Are you now? What're you two gonna do?"

"Probably just get lunch. It's only sixteen students, so I might as well get to know a few of them before we're stuck together all summer."

"What's his name?" I take a drag, holding the cigarette between my lips. Somewhere in the distance, I can hear a car alarm going off.

"Rory." She leans her head back again to look at me. "He actually reminds me of you a bit."

"Yikes. One of me is bad enough!"

Our laughter spooks a few birds from the trees around our little clearing, which only makes us laugh harder. After a few more quiet minutes, we decide to head back down to the car.

By the time we get back to her place, the sun hangs low in the sky, kissing the horizon. We shower together, Amelia making the same joke she always does about saving water, then kick back on her bed in our underwear, letting the warm breeze coming through her window tickle our skin. We bicker about what to watch until she decides we're watching *Gossip Girl*. But the show goes unwatched as our lips meet and our bodies coil together under the light of the setting sun and the TV. My phone sits on the nightstand buzzing away, unnoticed.

ONE

I'm staring at a painfully blank screen, wishing this essay would just write itself. I kick myself for agreeing to do this for Amelia, but there weren't any other options. Asking me to write her first conservatory assignment last week was the first time we'd spoken since the hike, and saying no would've meant her disappearing again. After a few outline sessions over the phone, it's time to finally draft the damn thing. Five hundred words on why art is important.

Talk about vague.

I check the time on my phone. Five-thirty. I need to get a first draft done now. I promised Devon we could go out to our friends' house party as our last hurrah before graduation tomorrow morning, and Amelia told me we'd meet up the night after graduation to revise and rewrite her essay.

And tell her I love her.

The page screams at me with deafening emptiness. Tomorrow can't come fast enough.

I push a few words onto the screen: *What is art? What isn't? How can we tell the difference?*

Fuckin' brilliant. Does this thing need a title? It should have a title.

My fingers hover over the keys, eager to jot down more, but nothing comes. Not a single thing. My brain is empty. Every thought I have ever had has been chased away by this slightly less empty page. The cursor blinks expectantly. I feel like I'm disappointing this tiny piece of code someone else worked very hard to create.

A little inspiration's all I need. Some music or something.

I open YouTube and scroll through my recommended music for... what? Blink-182? The Format? The Decemberists? And on and on, endlessly.

Too many choices. Just pick something.

I click on the search bar, popping up the cursor again. I get the feeling it likes watching me struggle to choose. Why does my brain have to disappear on me now? Writing my own papers is no problem; why is it so much harder to do for someone else?

"Welp," I say aloud to my empty bedroom, "I tried." I close my laptop and push it off my lap onto the bed next to me. I pull my phone out and look up some porn.

At least this'll be productive.

The website loads up as I lie down and shimmy my pants off. I swat the half-filled journals and pens off my nightstand and grab the box of tissues I keep nearby for... emergencies. I drop the blinds on the window next to my bed and pick a video.

No free shows, even for the neighbors.

As I'm getting into the groove, a phone call comes up, ringtone blaring. It's Amelia. I pull my hand out of my underwear and pick up.

"What's up?"

"Are you doing something right now?" Her voice sounds tinny and distant. She's driving somewhere while I'm on speaker.

"Not anymore." I tuck my disappointed erection into my waistband and sit up. "What can I do for ya?"

"So, change of plans. Can we meet up tonight instead of tomorrow?"

"I mean, it's not ideal. I haven't finished the first draft yet, plus I'm supposed to hang out with Devon tonight—"

"Aren't you two going on a road trip right after graduation? Just hang out then." She lays on the horn. "Pick a fuckin' lane, asshole! Sorry."

"Please be careful. You should focus on the road." I get up and pace the small, clean path from my bed to my door.

We always have to work around her schedule.

"I'm fine. And we can just do the draft together. That way I can look over it and make sure it sound like something I'd write." Her voice shows no indication she recognizes how inconvenient this change of plans is.

"Okay, but I'd still prefer if we just met up tomorrow."

"I can't do tomorrow. I'm meeting up with Rory again. It was sorta last minute. We—" The sound of another car horn cuts her off. "What do you want me to do? It's a fucking red light! Look, Jared, I gotta go. I'll be there around eight, okay?" She hangs up before I can say anything else.

With a frustrated sign, I sit down and drop my phone onto the bed next to me. Amelia always does this.

Why does she have to hang with Rory tomorrow? And what the fuck am I gonna tell Devon?

A knock at my door makes my stomach drop.

"Go away!" I hop off my bed, almost landing face-first in one of several piles of dirty laundry scattered around my small bedroom. "I'm... masturbating!"

The door cracks open. Devon pokes his head through. "Bullshit. You wouldn't have answered if you were whacking off."

"You know me too well." I shovel an armful of laundry into the corner between my dresser and desk, being sure to avoid eye contact. "What do you want?"

"Are you actually cleaning your room?" He walks in and puts a hand against my forehead. "You feelin' alright?" He laughs as I pull my head away from his hand. "No, I came to see how you're doing. Make sure you're sufficiently *jazzed* for the party tonight." His excitement bristles in the air like static.

God, I am such an asshole.

Between finals and Amelia's essay, I haven't had any time to hang out with Devon, and he's been bummed as hell about it. Lately, he's been spending most of his free time on the phone with his family instead of going out, which makes me feel bad. Plus, he tells me going out alone just isn't the same, which makes me feel even worse.

"Jared? You in there?"

I look up from the growing laundry mound in the corner. "Yeah, I'm here. Sorry, just... distracted. This essay is stressing me out."

Devon moves to my bed and sits down. He kicks an old pair of underwear at me. "I don't understand why you agreed to write that essay for her in the first place."

I had to find a way to get her to make time for me.

"Just being nice." I grab the boxers in another armful and toss it all on the growing mound. "Besides, she's paying me to do it."

"Is she really?"

No.

"Course she is."

"It doesn't matter, dude, even before this. Seems like she's very keen to reach out when she needs help with work."

"I like helping her; it usually gives me an excuse to spend the night too."

"Like you need an excuse." Devon looks over the small collection of liquor bottles I keep next to my nightstand. He grabs the bottle of Jameson and takes the last swig. "Have you talked to her yet?"

I go back to the mound, dropping a few loose socks on top like skiers from a helicopter. "I'm going to after we finish up tonight." The words are out before I catch myself.

"What'd you mean? We're going out tonight."

I stiffen as the energy in the room shifts from excitement to confusion. "Well, here's the thing—"

"No. No fuckin' way." His voice is harsh but not angry. Not yet, anyway.

"Well, Amelia called me a little while ago, before you came in, and asked if she and I could meet up tonight instead."

"And you told her no, right? Because we're going out." His gaze hardens as my mouth goes dry. "Jared, you told her no. Right?"

"What was I supposed to do, Devon? This is—"

He buries his face in his hands and leans forward, elbows on his knees.

"You know this is my last chance!" My voice is loud, anxiety sublimating into anger.

He rubs his face with his palms before dropping them. He inhales but stops the words from coming out by tightening his mouth into a taut line.

"We have an entire road trip ahead of us! So what if we don't go out tonight? We're gonna be out every night for the next three weeks. We're gonna have a whole week in New Orleans getting wasted, partying, exploring, whatever we want! I don't understand why this is such a problem!"

Without a word, Devon stands up and walks to the door. With his hand on the doorknob, he turns and stares me down with hard eyes. His voice is ice-cold, measured, and even. "You are more than welcome to stay here. *I* am going out to celebrate, with or without my *best* friend. I guess I'll see you when I see you."

He slams the door behind him, leaving me to feel like an absolute piece of shit.

By the time Amelia texts me to let her in, my raging self-hatred has mellowed into a tepid self-loathing. She greets me at the door with a beaming smile and a huge hug.

"Go put my bag in your room. I have to go back to the car for something." She hands me her L.L. Bean backpack before walking back out.

I set it down next to the bed and look around my room. Besides the overflowing trash bin and the mountain of laundry almost up to my chest, the room looks almost habitable. I pull my fuzzy blue slippers out from their hiding place under the dresser and slip them on. Amelia'll steal them if I'm not wearing them. Speaking of almost habitable... I poke my head into the adjacent bathroom. Looks clean enough: no hairballs in the shower or sink, toilet seat's down. Good thing it looks all right; I forgot to check it before.

A look of horror spreads over Amelia's face as she walks inside. "When's the last time you cleaned in here, Jared? Jesus Christ."

"I know, I know. I was gonna clean up more tomorrow before you got here, but obviously..." I let my voice trail off as Amelia's phone chirps. She sets her laptop bag down against my dresser and pulls out her phone. I sit on my bed, watching her tap away. Her eyes meet mine after a minute or two.

"This is for you, by the way." She crosses the room and hands me a large brown paper gift bag. "A little surprise."

Amelia *loves* surprises: surprise messages, surprise gifts, and, of course, the occasional surprise adventure. Something about catching people off guard must give her the warm fuzzies, but I hate them. I've hated them ever since my parents got *surprise* divorced when I was ten. But Amelia's surprises are the one exception. Her surprises usually make me smile and don't take years of therapy to cope with. The last gift was a sandalwood and bergamot candle for my room because she said it smelled like stress and ball-sweat. I told her that's why we hang out at her place.

"What's this for?" I ask, but she doesn't answer because she's sat down at my desk and buried her face back in her phone.

I turn my focus on the tissue paper popping out of the top of the bag. Pulling it out, I wad it up and toss it at Amelia. It bounces harmlessly off her head, pulling her attention back to me.

"Don't you wanna see me open it?"

"Just let me send this message. Okay, Butthead?" She taps away for a few more seconds before tucking her phone back in her pocket. She folds her hands in her lap and cocks her head to one side. "Ya gonna open it or what?"

Inside the bag is a box. I take it out and hand the bag back to her. It's already been opened, the top flaps folded over one another to reseal it.

"What is it?" I hold it up to my ear and gently shake it.

"How 'bout you open it up and look?"

"You are so *helpful*."

I pull apart the flaps and reach inside. My fingers find leather and paper. I pinch and lift out a dark green journal. It's small, about the size of two decks of playing cards placed next to one another, but it's beautiful. The leather cover has a nautical compass rose embossed on it, and a little ship's wheel charm hangs from an attached leather cord. And the pages. They're thick and brown, with a coarse texture unlike any paper I've ever used. It would be perfect for jotting short poems in after a hike or keeping dreams in so they can be remembered when life gets unbearable.

"Amelia, this is..." I look at her, expecting to see that radiant smile beaming at my joy, but she isn't smiling at me. She's smiling at her phone. "Amelia."

"Yes!" Her head snaps up from whatever she's typing. Her face goes from surprised to confused to concerned as she sees the journal in my hand. "I thought I put the other one on top! They must've gotten jostled around."

She snatches the journal from my hand and sets it on the desk behind her before pointing to the box. "Yours should be on the bottom."

I reach back in and pull out another journal, exactly the same as the first, but in a deep, royal blue. My favorite color. I twist the ship's wheel cord around my finger.

"I love it, Amelia." I leaf through the pages, feeling their rough weight.

"The guy at the stationary store said this paper would be better for your fountain pens. I remember you saying they always bled through your normal notebooks and stuff, so I wanted to get ones that wouldn't happen with."

I can't believe she remembered that. I can barely remember that. Her asking me why my notes were always so messy while getting dinner with me to go over what she missed in class that day. That would've been... first semester, junior year?

"But why'd you get one for yourself then?"

"First off," she gently kicks my leg, "you're welcome, Butthead."

"Right. Yes. Thank you."

"Second, I figured you could do some writing on your trip, and I could do some at my conservatory, then we could swap next time we see each other. That way we'll always have a little piece of each other. But you gotta promise me you'll write in it, okay?"

"I promise."

I lean off the footboard of my bed and grab my satchel bag off its wall hook.

"I'll even put it in with the rest of my road trip stuff, so I can't forget it." I set it in and buckle the bag closed. "Thank you, Amelia. Seriously. It's wonderful.

Before she can say anything, her phone goes off again.

"When are you leaving again?" She swipes her phone open and begins typing away.

"Devon's flying back to Arizona tomorrow afternoon after the ceremony, then I'm heading out early morning Saturday."

She doesn't answer for a few seconds, then speaks again without looking up. "Are you excited to have your own car?"

"We'll be splitting it, but yeah, I'm excited. It'll be nice driving to work, especially since the bus stops nowhere near my new job." I fall back on my bed, annoyed by her fixation on whoever she's texting. "I'd rather stay here with you, though."

She lets out a boisterous laugh. "No, you wouldn't! I'm gonna be busy as shit working with Rory and everybody else in my program. I wouldn't have any time to do anything!"

"Is that who you're texting?" I can hear the edge in my voice. I hope she doesn't.

"Yeah, we've been talking and seeing each other a lot over the last few weeks."

Great. Guess that's why she's been so hard to get a hold of.

"But seriously, if I stay, we can go on car rides, watch those *terrible* rom-coms you kept trying to make me watch. Shit, I'll even cook for you if you'd like. It'll be just like the last two years, but even better."

I wish I could tell you just how badly I want to be with you.

She looks up from her phone and smiles that smile I love. That smile could warm the vacuum of space. She stands up and kicks her shoes off.

"You're such a butthead," she says as she climbs on the bed next to me. "You've got your trip with Devon. And you're gonna have so much fun. I doubt you'll even be thinking about me." Hearing her say his name makes those gross feelings bubble up inside me, but I keep it to myself.

Amelia rests her head on my chest, listening to my heart beat. I can feel her torso expand and contract with every even, steady breath. Her hair smells like lilacs and clean linen.

Can we stay like this forever?

"Should we get started on my essay?"

Her voice is so delicate, it barely breaks the silence. I take a deep, slow breath, letting the last few quiet moments with her against me sink in. I shift to sit up and pull the laptop out from under my leg.

"I didn't get through much."

"Good thing I brought snacks then."

TWO

"For someone who claims to enjoy writing as much as you do, you're pretty shit at it."

I peek over my laptop screen at Amelia, laying half-off my bed, feet on the floor. In one hand, her phone; in the other, a snack-sized bag of Cheetos. I lift a few Cheetos from my own bag into my mouth and crunch them loudly. We've been at this for two hours now.

"This might go faster if you took your nose out of your phone and actually helped me."

"Can't we just jump to the part where it's finished?" She pouts, turning to look at me for a moment.

"If I jump while I'm eating, I might choke." I dump the remaining Cheetos into my mouth, ball up the bag, and toss it at the bin. It bounces off the other trash and rolls near the door. I look for a giggle, a smile, any kind of recognition for my joke. But no laughter comes, no smile. Just the light glow of the screen reflecting off her stony face.

My stomach tightens.

Is it still Rory? It's got to be.

"Hey, Amelia?" I nudge her snacking arm with my foot.

"What's up, Butthead?" Her eyes flick over to me.

Stop staring at your fucking phone and talk to me.

"I wanted to ask you about some—"

I'm cut off by her phone's shrill ring. Her eyes dart back to the screen as she sits up.

"It's Sarah."

I give her a surprised look. Sarah's the one hosting the party Devon and I were supposed to go to. Well, Sarah and her house mates, Jess and Kat, are hosting. All three of them are juniors, so this is their way to say goodbye to all their senior friends and classmates. Sarah and Amelia met in class about a year ago and became fast friends.

"It's gotta be, what? Ten-thirty?" I check my phone for the time. "Yeah, I figured she'd have her hands full with the party by now."

She shrugs and picks up the call. I push my laptop off me and slide across the bed to sit behind her as she talks. I scratch up and down the length of her back, letting her words wash over me. No, not even the words. Just her voice. Like a tidal wave of fleece, it surrounds me, powerful and gentle.

Please, God, don't let me blow this tonight. I'll do whatever you want. I'll give up so many things for Lent. I'll stop cursing, I'll even go back to church and start believing in you again. Just give me this one thing. Please.

Amelia turns to me and points at the phone with her other hand. I have no idea what she's trying to get me to do. I furrow my brow in confusion, drawing an exasperated look from her.

"Do you wanna say hi?" she mouths.

I wrinkle my nose, but she insists, offering me the phone. With a groan, I pluck it from her hand and press it to my ear.

"What's up, Sarah?"

Amelia swats at my outstretched leg. "Be nice," she whispers.

"That *was* nice."

"Jareeeeeeeeeeed!" Sarah's voice squeals out of the phone. She's totally fucked up, screaming over whatever EDM they're blasting. "Where are you?" Her words slip and slide into one another like children on a frozen pond.

"I'm at home, Sarah. Working."

"I know! Devon told me and Kat you were... I don't remember what he said!" She bursts out laughing so loudly I have to pull the phone away from my ear. I give Amelia a pained look. She giggles. "But you should come over!"

"I can't. I'm helping Amelia with some work...."

"Wait... You're with Amelia, like, right now?"

I bite my tongue. "Yep, and I'm gonna give you back to her now."

"I miss youuuu!" she wails as I pass the phone back to Amelia.

"Hi, Sarah. So how much more do you need?" She listens as Sarah babbles something I can't make out. "Yeah, let me check. Some of them might still be in my car."

Before I can ask what's up, Amelia's up and out the door with my damn slippers.

"Where are you going?" I call after her.

No reply. The backdoor opens and shuts. My neck tenses up.

Oh, God, something's about to go wrong. No, something is already wrong. This is what I get for waiting until the last second.

Before I work myself up too much, the door opens and shuts again. Amelia says goodbye to Sarah as she comes back into my room, her jacket hung over her arm, and sits at my desk.

"I gotta do a thing. I'll be back later." She grabs her shoes and starts pulling them on.

I should've told her on the hike.

"Whoa, hold up. Where're you going?"

"Sarah had me run out and buy booze for them earlier, so I also picked up a few things for myself." She knots the first shoe, tugging on the second. "But they're almost out, so she offered to buy some of my bottles." She stands up and grabs her backpack.

"When are you gonna be back?"

"Not sure. Keep working. I'll see you later." She opens the door and walks out into the hall.

Great. Now what? I can't go to the party with her. If Devon sees me there, with Amelia, he'll shit my pants. But if she comes back late, or doesn't come back at all... Damnit.

I'm on my feet before my nerves can stop me. "Amelia! Hold up!"

I throw open my dresser, rummaging around for something decent to wear in public. My heart hammers in my chest.

This is a terrible idea.

I struggle pulling off my white T-shirt and raggedy sweat pants. My skin is hot and already slick with nervous sweat. I climb into a pair of black jeans, a gray T-shirt, and a red-black plaid flannel button-down. Hopefully, I won't have a heat stroke. I need socks. I open the top drawer and find none.

Where the fuck are all my socks?

Scouring Laundry Mountain, I grab the first pair I find. They're black and white, like a cow. I almost trip pulling them on. My breaths are shallow and fast. I feel dizzy. I race out the door, shoes in hand, and try not to fall down the porch steps. I run over to Amelia's car, which is thankfully still in the driveway. Throwing open the passenger door, I hop in and buckle up. She doesn't even look shocked.

"I thought you'd already left."

"I waited." She flashes that sweet smile. Another pleasant surprise. We back out of the driveway and head to Sarah's as I slip on my shoes.

The cool wind on my hot face feels nice as we drive. I forgot to put on deodorant before we left, so hopefully, I don't smell. My leg bounces rapidly as I watch the familiar trees and buildings flit past, illuminated by the streetlamps and floodlights. Amelia's put something on the radio, but I don't recognize the song. The music is drowned out by the wind from the open window.

"Jared, you okay?"

Her question pulls my focus back inside the car.

"Yeah, I'm fine."

"You're clenching."

She nods at my balled-up hand, knuckles white from squeezing, on the center console. I hadn't even noticed. I flex my fingers out, releasing my death grip on myself. Only then do I realize how tense I am.

"I'm nervous." I look down. Amelia's always been the outgoing type. I'm convinced she doesn't even know what nervous is.

"Why would you be nervous? It's just a party. You've been to plenty of those. And a bunch of people you know'll be there." Her words are comforting but do little to unspool my coiling tension.

"That's the problem. Devon's gonna be there. If he sees me at the party with you, he'll shit."

"Why would he care? We hang out all the time, don't we?"

"'Cause he wanted us to go to the party, but instead, I bailed to work with you." I look up from my lap. Amelia stays fixated on the road. "So, if he sees you and me there, together, he's going to shit."

She says nothing, letting my statement hang in the air like a bad smell. She glances at me from the corner of her eye. She sets her hand on mine and gives it a small squeeze. "I know just the thing. Grab my backpack from the back seat."

Her attention returns to the road as we come up to a red light. I twist around and grab her bag. Setting it on my lap, she unzips it and feels around.

"What're are you...?"

Her face lights up, and she pulls out a half-full plastic water bottle.

"Hold onto that." She tosses the bottle to me. "And put my bag back."

"I appreciate it, but I'm not terribly thirsty."

"That's fine, Butthead. Save it for when we get to 7-Eleven."

I shoot her a confused look as the light turns green and we turn left. I feel like a dog being driven to the vet. I stare at the plastic bottle, crinkling it gently in my hand. The liquid inside rises and falls like a sleeping man's chest.

Before I know it, we're pulling into a parking space, the bright green and white sign smiling down on me. Amelia turns the car off and hops out. I set the bottle in the cupholder before unbuckling my seatbelt and climbing out after her. The tension in my legs releases as I take a few steps, but my neck and shoulders remain taut. I stretch my arms up tall as I round the car. She's waiting by the trunk, her hand outstretched. I take it.

"Which flavor you gonna get?"

"I'll see what they have."

"I'd recommend blue raspberry. It'll cover the taste of that cotton-candy vodka when you mix 'em."

So, that's what's in the bottle. What can I say? The lady knows me.

We walk over, and I hold the door open for her. The Slurpee machine purrs eagerly as we approach. Its four icy cylinders roll and toss their sugary contents. Amelia grabs two large cups and hands me one.

"Cherry Coke is my go-to gal." She winks at me as she pulls the third lever. Her cup fills with sweet, brown slush. I tug the first lever, releasing a torrent of electric blue ice into mine. She hands me a lid and a long, red plastic straw with a shovel on the end that always slices the corners of my mouth. Amelia pays, and we head back out to the car.

I suck down a big gulp of the freezing drink, letting it cool my insides and wash the nervous, bitter taste out of my mouth.

Amelia takes the bottle from the cup holder and unscrews the cap. "How much you want?"

I take another sip to make room and pop the lid off. "Just dump the whole thing in there. It's way too sweet."

"That's the spirit!"

I swirl the half-melted mess to mix it together. It smells like fruity gasoline and probably tastes like shit, but now isn't the time to be picky. I press the lid back on and suck two big mouthfuls through the straw. I shudder.

It definitely tastes like shit.

"How is it?"

"It'll do the job." I take another sip and shudder again. Amelia laughs, and I realize she hadn't checked her phone since we left the house. A smile grows across my face.

"Fuck yeah, let's roll!" She turns the car on, and I roll all of the windows all the way down. I connect my phone to the radio.

A little alcohol and a little loud music. I can do this.

I blast some Green Day as we tear out of the lot toward the party.

THREE

When I was little, I had this recurring nightmare about being stuck underwater. Didn't know how or why I was there, but I needed to get to the surface, obviously. It was bright, so I couldn't have been too far down, but the water was murky as hell. Panic would set in, and I'd spin in circles, looking desperately for something to save me. Then, this flash of clarity would cut through the panic. If I figured out where the light was coming from, I could just follow that to the surface.

There was nothing else in the water to throw me off, so I'd just start kicking toward the light. Every second made my lungs burn a little hotter, but sure enough, I could start to make out little flickers and ripples in the light. My vision would start to vignette, but I was so close, I just had to breach, and I could have as many deep, cool breaths as I wanted. What I reached wouldn't be the surface, though. Only these huge, polished mirrors reflecting light from the surface. Fear would saturate my every thought, leaving me to ruminate on my final mistake before I'd bolt upright and yell for Mom.

Standing on the stoop, doorknob in hand, I wonder if I'm going to drown in this party too.

"You alive in there, Butthead?" Amelia pokes my butt with her elbow. "You got this!"

"Are you sure I can't steal a little from one of those bottles?" I ask over my shoulder.

"These are bought and paid for. I'm sure somebody'll pour you a drink inside, but you have to *open* the door."

I can already hear the sound of people seeping out of the house like ooze.

"You know I *love* hot, cramped, loud places." I let out a short breath and twist the knob.

Immediately, I'm hit with ear-splitting music and party funk. That unmistakable blend of sweat, powdered Kool-Aid, and weed punches me square in the face. I wrinkle my nose as Amelia steps onto the landing next to me.

"Get the door, or all the A/C will get out!" The music is so loud, Amelia still has to yell despite leaning into me.

"I'm pretty sure it's cooler outside!"

She nudges my arm and smiles. Her confidence everything will be fine is refreshing. She may be a huge pain in the ass sometimes, but she sticks with me.

"I'm gonna go find Sarah, okay? Try and have a little fun!"

I nod, putting on a brave face. She nudges me one more time before heading up the stairs into the living room. She hoists the bottles over her head, making the crowd whoop and holler with excitement.

With Amelia gone, I scan the crowd, making sure I don't see Devon. Hopefully, Amelia doesn't bump into him either. A few weeks ago, he and I would've taken this party by storm. We'd roll up, a bottle of Jameson each, with no plans but getting completely and utterly destroyed while making great memories neither of us would remember. Thinking about it now makes me feel guilty for bailing on him—and nervous for rolling up without him.

The song finishes, a moment of quiet descending on the party while whoever's in control of the music looks for their phone.

"Jared? What're you doing here?"

My head swivels from the upstairs crowd to the adjacent staircase leading to the basement. Swaying up the stairs is Jess, her pearlescent skin glowing in the rainbow party lights.

My first ever conversation with Jess was about genocide. We were both taking the same history elective, and we didn't talk much until we got paired together to represent Ukraine in the mock UN session we were doing as our final. We spent several meals and a few evenings together, planning our case and legal propositions, only to get utterly steamrolled by Russia in the session. Afterward, we stayed in touch. When I wasn't too busy with Amelia, she would drive us out to this small whiskey bar she knew so we could shoot the shit in peace. I even saw her in a play one time. She's a theatre student, like Amelia. I usually kept our hangouts to myself, though, since Amelia would give me shit for it. Maybe she was jealous. Who knows?

Jess is wearing a light blue summer dress with little birds on it. They might be sparrows, but I'm not really sure because my eyes keep drifting from the birds to the low-cut neckline. My brain tells my eyes to move, but they don't.

She's going to notice I'm staring.

The telling becomes screaming as she gets closer, but the vodka Slurpee is making my internal workings a little slow.

Not even two minutes in, and I'm making an ass of myself. A new record.

"A friend of mine dragged me out." My eyes finally manage to break orbit from her chest as she joins me on the landing. "I like your dress."

Of all the things, that's what comes out? Really?

"I noticed," she says flatly.

My face flushes red while my stomach does a kickflip. I let out a small, forced laugh and pray I don't get punched in the mouth. Her gaze softens as she laughs too. A wave of relief breaks over me.

"I got it from a thrift shop on the upper east side. I just *had* to have it 'cause it fit so perfectly." She does a little twirl; the bottom hem catches air and spins up in a whirl of soft, blue fabric as blood rushes from my brain to my dick.

"It certainly does!"

Just shut the fuck up. Please.

She gives me a coy look, a little smirk forming at the corner of her mouth. The music starts up again, forcing us closer together to hear each other.

"You don't have a drink."

"Not yet! But I would very much like one."

I can't say stupid shit if my mouth is busy.

She passes me a flask I hadn't noticed her holding. I unscrew the cap and take a sip. It tastes like sugar-free peach rings dipped in acetone. It burns like hellfire, too, reflexively making me gasp after I swallow.

"Jesus Christ, what the hell is that?" I hand it back, eager to be rid of it.

"It's Kat's peach moonshine! It's so bad, I couldn't bear it alone."

The hot, vile liquid reaches my stomach, mixing in like poison.

"Happy to help share the burden, I guess." I wipe my burning lips with the back of my hand. "God, that shit's terrible."

"If you want, I've got some better stuff on the bar in my room."

The sound in the room falls away as the moisture leaves my mouth. She's got this look in her eyes I can't decipher. I'm not sure if it's just the party lights or the alcohol or something else entirely.

"I think..." My eyes flick from hers to the cluster by the top of the stairs. My heart is fluttering again.

Amelia did say to try and have fun. Besides, she's probably busy texting Rory or whatever. Devon won't be able to find me, either.

"I'd like that," I finally say.

Her smirk unfurls into a sharp smile. "Come on then."

I follow her down the stairs into another undulating crowd, unable to shake the feeling I'm getting further and further from the surface.

Jess leads me down a short hallway and into the main basement room. We weave through exuberant partiers and slip into her room. The music is quieter in here, so we don't have to yell at one another. I let out a long breath.

"You all right?" Jess hands me a plastic tumbler before plucking one from the stack for herself. The stack sits on her bar, a three-tiered, dark wood cart filled to the brim with bottles of all sizes, shapes, and colors. Truly a sight to behold.

"Not a huge fan of crowds." Her incredulous look makes me chuckle. "I know. Weird, right?"

"Why do you go to so many parties if you hate crowds?" She plucks a bottle off of the bar and uncorks it.

"If I'm outside, it's fine. I can do concerts and shit like that, no problem. But indoor crowds? No way." I accept the outstretched bottle and pour myself two fingers of dark brown nectar.

"Tell me if you like this one."

I take a sip. It's proofy, brown-sugar sweetness with notes of vanilla and baking spice.

"Now, *that* is a drink." I finish the glass in two more sips. "What is that?"

"Peerless," she reads off the bottle. "Kentucky bourbon."

"Could I have a little more of that?"

She pours another splash, and I greedily gulp it down.

We move from bottle to bottle, from bourbon to Irish, from eighty proof to cask strength. We drink and laugh and tell stories, making our way from standing around the bar cart to sitting on her bed. I tell her about my upcoming trip, about how excited I am to see the whole country, especially New Orleans and Bourbon Street. She hangs on every word, hopping up from time to time to grab another bottle for us to try.

"Do you have any Scotch by chance?" I finish my fourth glass, handing it to Jess. She stands, taking a moment to find her feet before walking to the bar. She hunts around for a bit before pulling out a large gray cylinder tucked behind some other bottles.

"This one—" She pulls the lid off and produces a large bottle wrapped in braided metal tendrils. "This one is special. I only break it out for celebrations."

"I mean, I graduate tomorrow. So, maybe…" I bite my lip and slowly extend my glass toward her. She takes it and sets it aside. Taking a clean cup off the stack, she pours two fingers of the liquid gold. I take the cup from her and bring it to my lips, letting the hot liquid roll over my tongue.

It tastes like honeysuckle and iodine, like a doctor's office in a blooming field. I swallow, feeling the heat radiate through my chest. I exhale; the breath passing over my soft palate is thick and tastes like smoke. I giggle, unable to contain my ecstasy.

"That might be the best thing I have *ever* put in my mouth."

"That is Bruichladdich Islay single malt Scotch whiskey. Aged fourteen years, I think." She pours herself a small glass and raises it. "Here's to new experiences!"

"Cheers!" I hoist my glass high, and we both drink. I set the empty glass on her nightstand and lie back. Jess sets her empty cup on her dresser and lays next to me, both of our legs hanging off the bed.

"Tell me something: Why don't you like *indoor* crowds?"

"You really wanna know?" I roll on my side, facing her, and prop my head up on my arm.

"Mhmm."

"My parents didn't love me enough." I struggle to keep a straight face as hers drops.

"You're so full of shit!" She swats at me playfully. "Seriously, why?"

"The first year after my parents got divorced, my mother decided we should do something special for Christmas. Every year, the local library where I'm from would become a proper North Pole, so Mom thought it would be fun to go get our pictures taken with Santa. Mind you, I'm eleven, and I know Santa isn't real, but she *insists* we go."

"Come on, that's kinda cute." She giggles, scooting herself an inch closer to me.

"So, we get there, and it's fuckin' packed. I mean, probably close-to-capacity packed. We waited in line for maybe forty-five minutes to get the pictures with Santa upstairs in the workshop. After that, she let me loose to explore the North Pole town area downstairs while she browsed. Well, I was trying to weave my way through a crowd on the stairs when some asshole hip checks me, and I go tumbling down twenty steps. I land on the ground, all disoriented and dizzy and shit. I had the wind knocked out of me, and I hit my head pretty good."

I push myself further onto the bed and lean over Jess's face.

"Everybody was staring at me, like this, unsure of what to do. I didn't recognize a single person in the whole group, so I started to freak out. Then, since I was basically concussed, I thought the ceiling was pressing down on me, and the crowd was pressing in on me, and I'd get squished. It was horrible."

I break away from her and lay back down, staring up at the ceiling.

"It only took my mom two minutes to get to me, but it felt like a lifetime. Never liked crowds after that. I don't mind them when I'm outside 'cause there's no ceiling, no impending threat of being crushed on all sides."

I stare up at the ceiling fan, fixated on a tiny dark spot on one of the blades. I let my eyes slip shut, feeling the room gently spin underneath me.

Maybe I'm that little dark speck, spinning around and around on the giant ceiling fan of Earth, always being moved but never actually moving.

Jess's hand brushes up against mine. I open my eyes and turn my head to see her.

"I guess I never got over it." A chuckle bubbles up inside me. "It's stupid, really."

I want to say more, to fill the silence between us, but my head is empty. No nagging thoughts or self-deprecating doubts. Just quiet, still space with Jess and me free-floating.

My eyes ask a silent question she answers with a kiss. My lips smile against hers as more chuckles bubble up in my chest. We push to sit up, our bodies coming closer together. She cups my cheek with her hand. Mine moves to hold the small of her back. Her glow seeps into me, burning away the terror that comes just before sudden intimacy. Her hands trace down my neck and move to the buttons on my shirt.

She tosses my flannel on the floor before pushing me onto my back. Straddling my hips, Jess presses herself into me. Our tongues twist and twirl as more clothing is tossed off the bed. The world falls away, leaving just the two of us. Our bodies join; two atoms in the sun's core, coming together to form something new, both brilliant and beautiful.

FOUR

Jess's hand feels soft under mine. Her head rests against my shoulder, hair a mess. Even though the room is unbearably hot, I don't want to pull away from her. Her bed is our own little island in an Earth-sized ocean, with nobody around who can bother us for miles and miles. It's just her and me, and that's enough.

"Sorry if my hand's sweaty."

She tilts her head back to look at me and bursts out laughing. "It's okay! Mine probably are too. It's like an oven in here."

She takes her hand from mine, reaching it straight up in the air. Her arm sways side to side like a palm tree, reaching toward the fan, before she drops it with a groan. She stares at me and pouts her lips a little.

I roll my eyes and exhale one breathy chuckle. "So smooth."

I slip my leg out from under hers and push myself onto my knees. My fingers fumble with the pullcord before finally finding purchase. The fan spins to life, cool air brushing our hot skin, as I roll back down to rejoin Jess. I shut my eyes, feeling the alcohol gently spin the world underneath us.

"I'm glad that friend dragged you out tonight," she coos.

"Me too." I trace small circles on her thigh with my fingers.

"And this can stay just between us. I don't wanna cause any problems."

I open my eyes and look down at her. "Sorry? What do you mean?"

"Well, I know you and Amelia are kind of a thing, and I don't wanna cause any drama or nothing."

Her name rips through my mind like a bullet. Instantly, the peaceful island is gone. I'm just in someone else's bed. Naked and vulnerable.

Amelia.

The warmth in the room turns icy cold as panic constricts my body like a python.

"You all right? You're squeezing my thigh."

Jess's voice sounds distant, like she's yelling down a tunnel at me. There's no air in my lungs to answer her, only ice water. I sit up and swing my legs off the bed. Snatching my underwear off the floor, I frantically pull them on.

"Gotta—just gotta use the bathroom." The words stumble from my lips and drop on the floor. I redo my pants and pull my shirt over my head, almost ripping the bottom hem out with a harsh tug. I grab my phone off the nightstand and cram it into my pocket.

"You remember where it is? Back down the hall—"

"—first door on the left, yeah." I shove my bare feet into my shoes and slip through the door, leaving Jess alone.

The basement looks like a shitty rave. Somebody set up some little laser and strobe lights on a shelf then turned all the normal lights off. EDM's blasting so loud my ribs are vibrating. Everyone's packed together, jumping and screaming like maniacs. My vision blurs as I'm swallowed into the crowd. Pushing through the writhing bodies, I mutter unintelligible apologies as I shove forward. I can feel everyone's eyes on me, can sense their knowing judgment and disapproval. I wish I could fold myself up like an origami crane, smaller and smaller until I disappear.

I break through a group of people who look excited to see me as I round the corner into the hall. I hope they have me confused with someone else. I shoulder-check the bathroom door open and dash in, slamming it behind me. I bang the back of my head once, twice, three times against the door, cursing myself.

What the fuck was I thinking?

I feel like I've been punched in the gut. No, like I'm still being punched with this huge fist, grinding deeper into my guts until it snaps me in half like a toothpick.

I move to the sink and splash some water on my face. I need to cool down and get this mess back under control. My stomach lurches and gurgles. I need to not puke. If I puke, it's game over.

If Amelia finds out about this, I'm fucked. All of our time together will have been for nothing, and she'll just go off with Rory or some other guy, and I'll be all alone. I'll have to get a cat or a dog to keep me company, but I'll still be miserable because I'm fucking allergic to both. Oh my god, I'm freaking the fuck out!

I press my face in my hands and massage my eyelids. Bright colors explode and dance as I force myself to take a deep breath.

"Pull yourself together, man!" My voice buzzes against my hands. I drag them down my face, catching sight of myself in the mirror. My eyes are all bloodshot, my hair's a mess, and I'm paler than the toilet. I look like an ancient, starving vampire.

I splash another handful of water on my face, then grab the hand towel to dry off. I stare at myself in the mirror, dead in the eyes.

What the fuck am I gonna tell Amelia?

Another wave of nausea catches me off guard. I throw myself at the toilet as vomit burns the bottom of my throat. My clothes are sticking to my skin as fresh sweat oozes from my pores, making me feel even more vile. Each drop is like a little ice cube sliding down my body, making me shiver. I pinch my eyes shut as I prepare for the night's drinks to make a reappearance. But after a few minutes of waiting, they don't.

I swallow a mouthful of saliva, making sure my body remembers which way liquids are supposed to go. I lift my head out of the bowl and open my eyes to see my savior: a half-full red solo cup sitting next to the toilet.

There is no way I'm this desperate.

The cup stares at me as if to say, "You are, and you know it."

With a shaky hand, I grab it and give it a sniff. It's fruity, definitely alcoholic. Probably the house drink.

Maybe one more drink will make this all better.

I bring the cup to my lips, but my hand refuses to tilt it up.

"Come on, Jared. You can't hide in here all night!" I whisper-shout at myself.

I pinch my nose and knock the drink down in three large swallows. It's way too sweet but does wash the lingering pre-vomit taste out of my throat. I toss the cup in the bin and take a deep breath. I feel like a crumpled ball of paper being unfurled.

I push myself back up to standing using the toilet bowl to keep me steady. I carefully step back to the mirror, giving my legs time to reboot. I run a hand through my hair, spiking it back to the appropriate level of messy.

"What are you going to tell Amelia? Nothing. You're finding Amelia and leaving." My reflection and I share a nod. I pull open the door to leave and walk straight into Devon.

Just by the look in his eyes, I can tell his brain is swimming in booze. In the three seconds it takes for me to metaphorically shit my pants, the mechanisms in his brain and mouth manage to establish a tentative connection.

"It *is* you! I thought I saw someone who looked just like you, but it is you!" He pauses to audibly suck a breath in over his teeth. "Wait, what're you doing here? I thought you had *other* plans!"

I bite my tongue and hope whatever lie is about to spill out of me will be convincing. "We finished! Blew right through, so I decided to catch a ride over."

His eyes blink separately as he works over my lie in his head. Hopefully, the alcohol has dulled him enough to buy it. He usually gets pretty empty-headed after the eyes-blinking-separately part.

"So, you didn't just come out with Amelia?"

"Course not."

I need to get out of here. I need to find Amelia and leave.

"In that case... do you wanna buy some shots?"

"I mean, I've already had a few. I'm not really—"

Devon throws his arm around my shoulders and marches me toward the stairs. "Come on, Buzzkill. One shot won't kill ya!"

Can I catch one break? Please?

"Fine, but only one. All right?"

He smiles a big, drunken grin, teeth and all, as I half-carry him up the stairs.

I scan every face as we push through the upstairs crowd toward the little bar set up in the living room. I can only pray Amelia has gone off somewhere else. If I run into her now, I'm boned.

Devon wrestles with his pocket to get his wallet out and slaps two singles on the makeshift bar.

"Two shots of whateveryagotleft." His words bleed together into an almost incomprehensible slurry. The bartender, a bigger guy sober Jared might recognize, nods and fills two little plastic shot cups. He sets them in front of us and scoops up the bills.

"What're we drinkin' to?" Devon asks me, hoisting his cup high. "Graduating?"

For a moment, that same guilt from earlier settles over my panic like a wet blanket. I feel bad for lying to him, for ditching him. This time last year, Devon and I were inseparable best friends, going to movies and bars in the city. We even went camping upstate that one weekend. But now, look at us. On the verge of our greatest adventure, our cross-country road trip, and I can't even tell him the truth about coming to a party.

It's only for a little bit, until Amelia and I are properly together. The road trip will be better.

"To better tomorrows." We tap cups and throw back our shots. My taste buds are so fried, I can barely taste anything but the alcohol.

"I like that one!" Devon sets his cup back on the bar and puts down another two dollars. "You remember when

I bought our first shots at our first college party? Waaaaay back, freshman year?"

"Yeah! We got that awful, watered-down blue curacao and thought it was so cool."

"And do you remember what you said it tasted like?"

"I wanted to say it tasted blue, but I thought to myself, 'blue, like a crayon, and Crayola makes crayons,' so I just said—"

"Crayola!" we shout together, falling into a fit of laughter. Two fresh shots are set in front of us.

I pick mine up. "Here's to Crayola."

"To Crayola!" We knock the drinks back. The alcohol burns my hard palate and throat on the way down, making me gag a little. Devon looks unbothered, lost in the hazy memories of countless parties.

"If you guys want, this is the last of 151 you've been drinking. Consider it a grad gift." He sets a full double shot glass in front of us.

A surprisingly wholesome gesture from a stranger? Are we in the backward dimension or something?

Devon thanks the guy and offers it to me.

"Riley's excited to see us," he says, sliding the drink my way.

Riley Gray, Devon's girlfriend, graduated last year and moved back home to Missouri with her parents to save money for grad school. We're spending a few nights at her place during our trip before hitting New Orleans. They met our sophomore year before we met Amelia. Their first date was a hike to one of the local parks, where Devon *allegedly* pushed her out of the tree they were climbing. To this day, she still insists Devon had tried to take her out while taking her out. She's as clever as she is wonderful. Devon's a lucky guy.

"Not as excited as you are to see her, I'd figure."

"What d'ya mean?"

I give another little gag after setting the empty bottle down. The last bit had been closer to two shots or so, I'd guess. Way more than I thought I'd be getting.

"Well, she's your girlfriend, yeah? So we'll probably do some group stuff when we get there, but you two will want most of the time for yourselves." I give him a cheeky look, and he blows a chuckle out his nose. "I figure I'll just hang around and try to do some writing or something; keep myself busy."

"We always try to include you, dude. You know that. A fulfilling relationship shouldn't replace your friends. We're not just gonna up and disappear on you." His head drops forward as he giggles to himself. "Like you almost did with Amelia tonight."

And to think, we were almost having a good time.

"You're right, Devon. Thanks for clearing that up." I give him a harsh, toothless smile and toss the shot glass at his chest. "And thanks for the shots."

The glass startles him as it bounces off his chest and into his fumbling hands. I merge into the surrounding crowd of dancing people and push toward the front door as Devon limply calls after me.

The night air cools my throat as it rushes into my lungs. I sit on the stairs up to the stoop, trying to push everything out of my head.

What a fucking nightmare tonight's turned into.

Being stuck in Devon's old Nissan as we haul across the country for three weeks feels so undesirable now. I bury my head in my hands, trying to cool my head after Devon's stupid remarks.

My head feels heavy and full of fog in the dark. Everything's spinning again, but faster. My stomach grumbles unhappily. The nausea's sneaking up on me again as the spinning continues to speed up. Panic rubs at the back of my brain.

I just wanted to have a good night with Amelia, but now I'm on this stoop, feeling disgusting because Devon just had to do shots with me. Whatever. Fuck him. Fuck this whole mess.

I make a grab at the railing next to me, my hand snatching at empty air before finding the metal. My vision swims as I pull myself up, instantly desiccating my mouth. I let go, letting myself plop back down on the stairs. If I try that again, I will one hundred percent throw up. A dim lightbulb flashes in my cloudy mind.

Text Amelia. She always makes me feel better.

I slap at my thighs, feeling for my phone. Getting it out feels like trying to solve a Rubik's cube. I open the screen and immediately get blinded. As I recoil, the phone slips from my trembling hands and clatters down the concrete stairs. It lands, screen down, on the brick walkway. I let loose a choice string of expletives. It's definitely out of reach now. I grab the railing and stretch forward as far as I can without getting up.

"Come on. You fuckin' piece of shit!" The railing's flakey, rusted metal scratches my palm, but it doesn't hurt. Small victories of being totally obliterated. "Come. On—"

"What the hell are you doing?"

The question startles me, and I lose my grip. I miss the steps entirely, landing on all fours on the walkway, right at Amelia's feet. She's smoking a cigarette with the phone pressed to her ear.

"Heyyy there!" I push myself back onto my butt and smile up at her. " I was gonna text you, but I dropped my phone."

"I'm gonna have to go," she says and hangs up. "Where's your phone, Jared?"

"Uhhh, behind you, I think." I close one eye and point past her leg. She picks it up and hands it to me. The screen is cracked but not destroyed.

"You look fucked up." She grabs my arm and tugs.

"No, standing makes me feel icky." I wiggle my arm out of her hand, letting it flop back down.

She raises an eyebrow at me. "Right. What're you doing outside?"

"Ran into Devon while hiding in the basement. Told him I came *without* you, which he was drunk enough to believe. We did shots, and then I felt gross, and now, here we are. What're you doin'?"

Amelia walks past me and sits on the stoop. I swivel around to face her.

"Well, I came back down to get you after chatting with Sarah, but you were gone. I got a drink and mingled, then I got a phone call, so I come out to smoke and answer it."

"Was it Rory?" My head rolls to my shoulder as I smile coldly.

"Does it matter?"

"Nah, I guess not."

My phone buzzes in my hand. It's from Jess. *Where'd u go?*

The color must've drained from my face because Amelia's at my side with barely enough time to darken the screen. Feeling her hand on my back lets me know this ordeal is almost through.

"You all right? Looked like you were gonna pass out there."

"Yeah, I'm... Do you think we can go back to your place now?" I put on my best I-don't-feel-well face, which doesn't look too much different than my face would normally after drinking this much, and hope she'll just whisk me to the car.

Instead, disappointment fills her face. "I was kinda hoping to get back in there. It's my—well, *our*—last chance to see most of these people for a while."

"Please. I don't—I can't go back in there." The softness in my voice surprises even me.

The disappointment in her eyes gives way as she pats my back gently. "Do you wanna say goodbye to anyone? Kat or Chris, or Jess, or—"

"I just wanna get out of here." Our eyes meet. For a moment, guilt sears my heart, but I keep my mouth shut.

Nothing is going to ruin this for me. Not Jess, or Devon, or Rory, or anybody. I have to tell her tonight before I leave, or I'll lose her. Three weeks apart is enough to deaden any heart.

She presses her car keys into my hands. "Remember where we parked? I'm going in to get you a bottle of water and say goodbyes." She takes my hand and pulls me up. My legs shake, but my vision stays stable enough for me to not instantly puke. "Can you make it?"

I nod gently as to not upset my already uneasy stomach any further.

"What would you do without me?" She chuckles, giving my hand a squeeze.

Fall apart?

"Hopefully, I'll never have to find out." I click the fob, listening for where her car is. "Don't take too long, or I'll puke in your trunk."

"If you puke in my car, they'll never find your body." She gives me a wink and heads inside.

I sway about a block down the street, looking around for her car. I click the key fob, looking for the flashing headlights. They blink three cars down from where I am. A sigh of relief rushes out of my mouth. I honestly couldn't remember where we parked, but I wasn't going to give Amelia the chance to take me back inside with her.

I climb in and buckle up, so I don't forget to later. A gurgle in my stomach works its way up my throat. Thankfully, it's just a burp. And what a burp it is. Had to be ten, fifteen seconds long! It shook the whole car. Amelia would've been jealous. Her record is eight seconds. I settle in to wait for her, confident the night will take a turn in my favor.

FIVE

Amelia comes back to the car with a weird look on her face. She turns the engine over and pulls out of our spot without saying a word. I run my dry tongue over my dry lips, desperate to generate some moisture in my barren mouth.

God, I'm parched.

"Did you bring me a water bottle?"

She says nothing, keeping her eyes fixed on the road ahead of her.

Guess not. I'll have a nice, cool glass when we get back to her place. She's got a Brita, too, so I know it'll hit the spot. Then we can curl up in her bed, and she can play with my hair, and I tell her I love her, and everyone will clap.

I set my hand on the center console, on top of Amelia's. She pulls it away before I can lace my sluggish fingers with hers. I try to make out her face, but the brief flashes from passing streetlamps give me little to work with.

Maybe she bumped into Devon, and he said something shitty. He can be such a prick when he's drunk.

Somehow, she still looks perfect, despite the chaos of the party. If I hadn't gone out with her, I would never know she'd been there. I could learn a thing or two about looking good after a party. It probably helps she doesn't drink much. Cuts down on that hammered-shit look.

"What're you staring at?"

"Your pretty face," I purr.

"Could you stop? It's distracting." She throws on her blinker and makes a right.

"Oh, man, *sorry*." I turn to look out the windshield. "Did you have fun?"

"Would've liked to stay longer." She looks over her shoulder before changing lanes. "But what can you do."

"I'm sorry."

"It's fine."

I open my mouth to continue the conversation but think better of it. I wouldn't be surprised if Devon said something mean to her. He's been so weird while I was working on her essay the last few weeks. All moody and shit. He *seemed* fine today. I just hope it doesn't ruin my shot.

"So, where'd you get off to?" Her voice is flat, toneless, and void of color.

"Made my way downstairs, looking for people to hang out with." I keep my eyes trained on the approaching red light. My knee is bouncing.

"Did you?" I can feel her eyes burning holes in the side of my head as we sit at the light. The car is starting to feel very small.

"Sat next to Kat on the couch. She gave me some of this horrible peach moonshine. Then I sat in the bathroom for a while because I felt gross." I shift uncomfortably, my stomach sloshing as I meet her gaze.

"That's so funny," she says with a smirk. The red light makes her eyes look like they're on fire. "I bumped into

Kat upstairs while Sarah went to get the money for me." The light turns green, but Amelia keeps staring through me. My heart thunders against my ribs so loud, I'm afraid she can hear it across the car.

"Oh, must've been someone else then."

"Yeah, must've been." She turns back to the road and starts driving, leaving me to vibrate with anxiety unexamined. She doesn't say anything else, but she really doesn't have to. I know I'm pretty much fucked. We sit in silence as we continue toward Amelia's house.

We pull into the driveway, and Amelia turns the car off. Rather than hop out, she folds her hands on the steering wheel and keeps staring through the windshield.

I am so going to regret this.

"Are you okay?"

"I'm trying to understand why you're lying to me."

My heart leaps into my throat. "I'm sorry?"

"You heard me." Her voice is completely dead. No inflection, no emotion, nothing. It's like she is reading a Chinese food menu out loud.

"I'm not understanding what you're..." My voice trails off as she lets out a big, frustrated sigh and starts fussing with her pocket. "What are you doing?"

She pulls out a wadded ball of... cloth? She holds it up for me to see, and my stomach drops as I do. It's not a wadded ball; it's socks. A pair of black and white socks, patterned like cow spots. The same ones I wore out tonight. The same ones Amelia got me for my birthday last year.

"Where did you—?"

"Bumped into Jess in the kitchen getting you a bottle of water. Said she was looking for you because you left *these* in her room. Any idea why she had them?"

"I don't fuckin' know, man. I'm drunk as shit. Maybe I got too hot—"

"You are so full of shit, Jared." She throws the sock ball at me. It bounces off my chest and lands on the floor. "She said you two were just hanging out in her room—whatever the fuck *that* means—and you just ran out on her without 'em."

"Jesus Christ, Amelia. What's that supposed to mean? I can't just be hanging out with someone in their room, right? I've always gotta be doing *something*, right?" My nerves start to catch fire, anger blooming in my drunken mind.

This is a losing battle; she's never going to believe me.

"Do *not* do that!" She's yelling now, and I can feel the adrenaline starting to kick in. "Do not victimize yourself! You were doing exactly what you do in a bedroom with one other person, with no socks on."

"No, I really wasn't!" My face is getting hot and red. My hands are bunched into tight fists, shaking with tension.

This isn't going to work. I should just tell her the truth before I say something I'll regret.

"Why can't you just be honest with me?"

"Why can't you be honest with *me*?" I scream, blood boiling. "What's the fuckin' deal with Rory, huh? You two are spending so much fuckin' time together. What's the deal with that, huh? I know you aren't doing work together because I'm doing all your fuckin' work, Amelia!"

She opens her mouth to speak, but I drown her out.

"No, *no*! Don't say a god damn thing. I can barely pull you away from your fuckin' phone while I am right next to you, working on your fuckin' essay. You have the audacity to come at me about this while you're flirting with some random fuck you've just met? What a fuckin' joke!"

I rip my seatbelt off and throw the car door open. I storm toward the front porch of her house. I need some space before I explode.

That wasn't the explosion?

Another car door opens and slams shut as Amelia comes after me.

"We can unpack all the hurtful shit you just said after you answer my—"

"We fucked, Amelia!" I turn on my heels to face her. If I'm hurling invectives, I might as well face the person I'm hurling them at. "Is that what you want me to say? We fucked. I'm sure it's nothing you and Rory haven't already done."

Amelia closes the distance between us. "It is midnight. Will you keep your fucking voice down?" she whisper-shouts in my face. Her whole body's shaking.

Am I shaking?

"And where is all this shit about Rory coming from? Why do you care *if* anything is happening? It's none of your business."

"Because I love you, you fuckin' idiot!" The words hit her like a brick in a pillowcase. Her eyes go wide as I continue unloading sentence after sentence straight into her face. "I've got this enormous you-shaped hole in my heart, and no matter who or what I cram into it, it never holds, because I am in love with you."

I sit on the porch steps. My legs are shaking too much to hold me up. Amelia just stares at me.

"Two years ago, you told me you didn't want a relationship, which was fine. I figured we'd just keep going strong until you were ready. I stopped hooking up with other people and waited so, so patiently for this moment, the moment where everything comes together, but now we're here, and it's... wrong."

I pull in a ragged breath that catches on a lump in my throat. I wish I had some magic words I could utter so all this would make sense to her. But there are none. There's just the maddening silence of Amelia watching me immolate myself.

"I pushed everything aside for you, for us. My work, my other friends, even Devon, because you are all I need. You complete me, Amelia. You make me whole. With you, I feel like I could conquer the world. But I could never... never *get* you. I don't know."

I drag my hands down my face, feeling the stubble gently scrape them.

"I had this dream we'd move in together, be a happy little couple, and everything else just falls into place. But all of a sudden, this other guy comes in and takes you away. I was scared. I *am* scared, and I needed my brain to be quiet. And Jess was there."

Amelia brings her hands together against her mouth. The streetlights behind her cast her face in shadow, but I can see the faint glint of moonlight in the tears on her cheeks. She's standing so still, like she isn't even breathing. I'd think she were a statue if she hadn't moved her hands.

I could really use those magic words.

"Will you please say something?" I can feel tears burning behind my eyes.

"What am I supposed to say?" Her mouth barely moves as she speaks, harsh and quiet.

I stand up, hoping to comfort her, but she steps back as I do. My heart sinks into my stomach, and my stomach onto the ground.

"You're not supposed to say anything. Just speak your mind."

Her eyes flick between mine and the yard around us as she searches for the right words.

"I think I need to be alone right now," she finally whispers, and I hear something small and delicate shatter inside me.

"Amelia, please—" I step toward her, reaching out to embrace her, to bring her close. "Just hear me out, please. Will you?" The words feel awkward in my mouth. I never thought I'd have to say them like this: Begging her to stay.

"There is nothing you can say right now to make this better." She gives me a wide breadth as she walks toward her house. I quietly pray none of her roommates are looking out their windows at us.

"Please, just... Wait a minute, let me—"

"Just stop, please."

I try to move toward her, but my legs feel like they're stuck in quicksand.

"I just need a second, Amelia. Please, just—"

"Jared!" Hearing her shout my name with such anger and sadness behind it instantly shuts me up. "I am asking you nicely to stop. I will not ask nicely again."

"What am I supposed to do?"

"I don't know. Go home; go somewhere else. I can't be around you right now."

I open my mouth, but she's inside before any sound escapes. The deadbolt slides loudly into place with a heavy, metallic click, leaving me alone in the quiet darkness.

SIX

I don't know what to do.

My brain is telling me to move, to get off Amelia's front lawn, to go home and faceplant in bed, but my body refuses. My eyes haven't finished seeing her slam the front door; my ears still ring with the lock turning over. I try to take a deep breath, but my diaphragm spasms and shakes. I feel like my guts have been extracted with a giant ice cream scoop and laid out on the grass in front of me.

I'm not ready for this.

I'm not ready to unlearn the feeling of her touch, the timber of her voice, the warmth in her eyes, the route from my house to hers, which I've walked countless times in the last two years. Our imagined future sears my soul like hot coals.

I remember Amelia and I reading Walt Whitman in a poetry class we took together. She loved his nature imagery, and I loved the profound beauty he ascribed to loss. "Nothing can happen more beautiful than death." Seems like a lifetime ago we read *Leaves of Grass*.

Seems like a load of bullshit now that I'm actually in it.

As the adrenaline drops off, my thoughts sink beneath the raging ocean of alcohol and distress. Suddenly, a drop of water lands on my nose, making me flinch. The gears in my neck release, my head falling back to face the sky. A few more drops plop on my forehead and cheeks. I almost can't believe it. I stare up into the charcoal black sky, dumbstruck at my picturesque misfortune. Tonight has proved quite the testament to my ability to be wrong.

My neurons manage to line up and fire off one clear thought through the haze: *I can't stay here.* This singular line of thought is immediately dogpiled by every other thought, seizing the opportunity to be heard before my head implodes.

What if this is it? What if I never see Amelia again? What if something happens to me on the walk home? What if I get mugged? Or hit by a car? What if they leave me for dead, pancaked against the street like roadkill? No, no, I don't wanna die! I can't do this!

My chest heaves as my brain fires off every flavor of panic it can muster. I rub my throat, trying to coax more air into my lungs through what feels like a half-pinched drinking straw. I need to get out of here. I need to quiet my head. I need a drink. I need a drink, and then another, and another until every frantic, painful thought is silent and dead.

The closest drinks are at home. If I hurry, I can probably get back with enough time to drink and fall apart before Devon gets there. I fumble for my phone, hands slow and numb from shock, and check the time. Just about quarter after midnight. Devon won't be home for a while.

I drag my hands down my face and shake them, casting off drops of rain and sweat.

At least I have a plan. Go home, get even more fucked up, and wallow until I pass out.

My shoulders are starting to feel wet, even through my undershirt. I look across the road at the streetlights. Little lines appear and disappear as they pass through the glow. I love watching the rain, waiting for the cracks of lightning and peels of thunder, but getting caught in it sucks shit. I tell my legs to start moving, but they refuse.

Okay. First step's always the hardest. Just gotta move some muscles to pull the bones. I've been doing this for twenty-one years now. Up, swing, down, repeat. It's like falling over, but very controlled, over a long distance.

Persuading my legs to work feels like performing some arcane ritual in a language I learned three days ago online. Finally, my leg foot comes up, and the first step follows.

One down, several hundred to go.

As my back leg swings forward, a wave of dizziness washes over me. I reel, feeling my balance start to go. My arms flap around like stapled-on noodles. I'm not sure if I'm doing that or if it's a reflex, but it helps, so who cares. Each step becomes easier as muscle memory kicks on, letting my brain focus on navigating. Grass becomes asphalt, and suddenly I'm standing on the street. My legs are already shaking like scared puppies.

What have I eaten today? Oh, yeah, a bowl of soup for lunch and Cheetos for dinner. Maybe I should have a real meal when I get home.

It's a fifteen-minute walk home if I hurry. Twenty if I take my time.

"This is gonna suck."

Saying it out loud makes me feel a little better. I puff up my chest and press on toward the main road. I'm on Maplewood right now. I need to get onto Route 112, follow it down a ways to the four-way intersection and my street, Ashford, cross there, and then I'm home free.

I can faceplant in my tiny, shitty twin bed. I wish my bed were bigger.

A fragment of a memory bubbles up to the surface of my mind as I walk. I let it burst and grow into a proper picture: A cozy, full-sized bed with clean, sky blue sheets. Sunlight spills into the room from a large bedside window and pools on my bare chest. The bedroom is clean; books on the bookshelf, clothes in the hamper, sheet music on the keyboard's rack.

I can hear the shower running and Amelia singing in the adjacent bathroom. She's trying to sing both parts to "Superboy and the Invisible Girl" from *Next to Normal*.

"Superboy and the Invisible Girl, she's the one you—fuck!" she shouts, having mixed up the first and second verses. I can't help but laugh at her incredible phrasing. She mumbles along for a second before jumping back in.

I stretch my arms out past my head and yawn big. My body shakes as the stretch deepens, until my elbow gives a satisfying pop. I exhale from the yawn and rest my arms on my chest, letting them soak up some of the warmth from the sun. It's Tuesday, so Amelia invited me over after my first class so we could hang out before Modern American Poetry. We were going to do some reading together, but we have a nasty habit of distracting each other, which I don't have an issue with, especially if she wants to be on top.

I sit up and eye some new photos hung on the wall behind her keyboard. She's got this string of fairy lights or whatever with little clips for small pictures between the LEDs. I walk over to get a better look at them.

Amelia out drinking with some drama friends.

Amelia at a formal with some dude she's definitely introduced me to whose name I can't remember.

Amelia and her family at a wedding of some kind.

As I scan over the rest of them, a pang of disappointment blooms in me.

She hasn't put any of us up.

We have plenty of pictures together, but they don't go on display. I know she keeps an old tissue box in her nightstand full of knick-knacks, photo booth strips, and movie tickets from our adventures. We called them "adventures" because she didn't want them to be dates. Amelia liked to maintain plausible deniability whenever we were in public together. I felt she was trying to hide me, but she always dismissed it when we were alone.

I sit down on the piano bench and pluck out a few sour notes. Amelia loves playing the piano. I started learning so we could play together, but I know my clumsy fingers slow her down, so I usually just let her play. She used to joke the two of us combined would make one great pianist because I can read the sheet music, and she can actually play it.

Amelia hits the money note at the end of the song, letting out a "fuck yeah!" as the music stops. Before the next song starts, I knock once on the wall and wait for her reply. Nothing.

Maybe she's got her head in the water or something.

I knock again, just once. Amelia knocks back once.

"You're doing it wrong!" I yell, hoping she can hear me through the thin-ish walls.

"I don't remember how it goes!"

"Ugh! What're you good for?"

"Absolutely nothing!"

I let out a belly laugh as the memory blurs and distorts like eight-millimeter film stuck in front of the projector bulb.

The rainy night returns to me like a specter, my focus shifting back to my surroundings. Route 112 is a fairly busy two-lane street with little shops, restaurants, and convenience stores up and down both sides. I've made it onto the sidewalk, in front of a split building, home to Domino's Pizza and Long Island Cycles.

Amelia and I rented bikes from this place last summer so she could teach me how to ride. Devon wanted to, but she made me promise no one else would. She told me biking's the closest you can get to flying without leaving the ground. We sent a video to my mom once I was able to stay upright on my own for more than a few feet.

My knees weaken as more memories start to break. Those plans we made to go biking through Central Park or the Hamptons seem so far away now. Not like we'll be going anymore. I massage at the knot in my throat. I back away from the building and rub my eyes hard, trying desperately to scour the images of imagined trips off my retinas with blasts of color. I turn away from the store, hoping to break the negative feedback loop. Across the street, I see the 7-Eleven we stopped at only two hours earlier. It feels like a lifetime ago now. Tears burn at the back of my eyes again. I bite my lip, keeping them at bay.

I can't do this.

Without a second thought, I drop my hands and start running down the sidewalk. My vision bounces like crazy as I try to stay focused on the ground ahead of me. If I trip, there's a good chance I won't get up. I'll just lie there and wait for the ground to open up and swallow me. Whatever is in my stomach sloshes audibly as I battle to stay upright against gravity's heavy hands tugging at me. Every footfall sends shockwaves up to my unstable core as I hurtle forward. My lungs are already burning, and I haven't even reached the first crosswalk.

Fuck, I'm so out of shape.

More buildings flash past me, their darkened glass storefronts reflecting a scared boy who can't outrun the beast nipping at his heels. As I come up to the first crosswalk, I don't bother looking for any traffic. The roads are all empty, anyway. My vision blurs again, black vignettes turning the crosswalk into a tunnel. I rush through without pause.

Back on the sidewalk, my lungs beg for me to stop, or at least slow down, but my legs aren't listening. They have their mission, and nothing is getting in the way.

Up ahead, the traffic lights on the four-way intersection come into view. The blinking red and yellow lights reflect in the rippling puddles and damp asphalt.

I'm so close. So, so close.

My heart threatens to punch through my ribcage like a starving monster eager to escape its cage. My messy hair has been flattened to my skull by the rain, hair product running down my face in thin rainwater trails. I just need to get across the intersection, and I'm there.

I push off my back foot, jumping over the stream running down the street toward one of the storm drains. My front foot lands hard, but I keep focus on the corner diagonal to me. I force whatever energy I have remaining to block out the pain in my legs as I continue my desperate sprint.

Halfway across, my front foot slips into an unseen pothole full of water, and I pitch forward at full tilt. My back foot loses traction, and I'm in the air before I've realized what's happening. My body spirals like a football through the air. I snap my eyes shut as my arms instinctively curl around my head. My shoulder hits first, the road biting deep into my flannel, followed by my arms and head. The wind is knocked out of me as I bounce once and skid across the wet road like a skipping stone. I stop tumbling and land flat on my back. I force my spasming diaphragm to work as I struggle to pull in a painful, labored breath. My arms come away from my head, sending pain shooting down into my chest. My eyes crack open, seeing a blurry mess of stars and streetlights. I try to lift my head to see if I'm as hurt as I feel but stop as hot pain sears up through my neck. My head falls back on the road as my vision vibrates and fuzzes away to empty blackness.

I hear Amelia shut the water off and pull back the shower curtain.

It's go time.

I sneak out of her room and down the hall to the bathroom. I pause outside the cracked door, listening. She's still got music playing.

All clear.

I delicately push the door open, just enough to peek through. Amelia's standing in front of the sink, one towel around her body while she dries her long, brown hair with another. She hasn't toweled the mirror off yet. I don't want to take my eyes off her, but the mission comes first. I push the door open enough for me to slip in. Once inside, I turn to shut the door, taking extra care to hold the slick doorknob steady so it doesn't squeak as it rotates back into place. Being caught this far behind enemy lines would mean a swift and summary execution. I turn back to see my target, Amelia, staring right at me.

Uh oh.

"D'you mind telling me what you're doing?" She puts her hands on her hips and cocks her head to one side.

"I do, actually. That information is highly classified, I'm afraid, so if you don't mind, I would like to finish my mission."

She smiles and shakes her head before turning back around to the mirror, a hand-sized swipe across it revealing how I'd been spotted.

I crouch and sneak up behind her, suddenly standing up and wrapping my arms around her waist. I rest my head on her shoulder. "How was your shower?"

"Hot and wet. Your favorite, Butthead." She winks at me in the mirror and pushes her butt back against me.

"Ooh, lucky me!" I kiss her cheek and catch a whiff of an unfamiliar scent. "Did you use a different shampoo?"

"I know, I know, it's not as good as the other one." She pouts. "But I haven't had a chance to hit the store."

"I like it! It's still good." I smile at her.

She rolls her eyes and chuckles. "You'd like anything on me."

"That's not true! If you lugged around a dead cat, I'd think that was kinda tacky."

"That's enough of that!" She makes a gagging sound and sticks her tongue out as she opens the mirror. She pulls out a tweezer. I lift my head so she can lean in closer to the mirror. She examines her eyebrows, pulling the left one taut first, then moving to the right one.

"How're the girls doing?" I love this little ritual. She always does this, and I swear, I've never actually seen her pluck a hair.

"They're doing good." She flicks her eyes to me for a moment. "My eyebrows are looking good too." She smiles, sticking her tongue out just a little bit to punctuate the joke.

"Oh, you," I say with cloying sweetness. " You are just *so* clever. Too clever for me."

"Oh, t'anks!" She says in a silly voice, making a big, dopey smile. She turns around in my arms and eyes my eyebrows. "Oh, yeah, you could use a weed whackin'."

"Absolutely not—" I drop my arms, but she catches me before I can escape.

"No, no, no. Sit!" She points to the toilet. I groan and do so, knowing she won't drop it if I don't.

"How bad can they be? You did them literally three days ago."

"Shush!" She straddles my lap and gets close to my face, rubbing my left eyebrow with her thumb. "We did your nose three days ago, not your brows."

"I'm not convinced." I fidget as she brings the tweezer up.

"Sit still, will ya?" she chides, hunting for an out-of-place hair to grab.

"Just make sure you actually get it out, yeah? Don't just tug the damn thing." I watch her face light up as she finds one.

"I always get them out." She jerks the tweezer back, and I feel nothing. "*Almost* always."

She tries again. This time, the pain is sharp and sudden.

"Shit my pants!" My hands fly up from my lap, but I stop them at my chest before I accidentally knock Amelia off me. She laughs hysterically as she eyes her catch.

"Getta load of that monster!" She holds the tweezer in front of my face. It's pinching a hair that's gotta be two inches long. "Where were you hiding that bad boy?"

I shrug as she rubs at the same eyebrow, looking for more prey. After finding nothing, she switches to the other one.

"I can't believe you forgot the knocks, *again*."

"I've been a little busy with all of my classwork and other shit in case—small pinch—you forgot." She plucks another hair, making me wince.

"Yeah, yeah, yeah, yeah, I get it. Pay attention." I wait for her to set the tweezers down so I know she's actually paying attention. "First knock." I knock once on the side of the cabinet under the sink. "That's 'Hey.'"

"Okay."

"Then, two knocks. That's 'What's up?' Okay?"

She nods.

"Three is 'I love you,' and four is 'I love you too.'"

"Okay, yeah, I remember this."

"Then do it with me."

Amelia and I alternate back and forth. Once, twice, thrice, four knocks.

"Now she's got it!" I smile at her as she beams.

"That's so cute." She kisses me on the nose, then grabs the tweezers.

I should've told her how I felt then.

A drop of water rolls down from my eyebrow and settles in my eye socket. I bring my hand to my face, slowly rubbing the drop away as my eyes flutter open. My hand is scraped to shit and bleeding a little. For a moment, I'm confused because I can't figure out why. Then another drop of water runs down my cheek and drips off my face. I look past my hand and see the traffic light hanging above me in front of the inky black sky. The thought finally connects, and my eyes widen. I bolt upright, causing pain to wash through my entire body.

I'm still in the street. How long have I...?

A throb from the back of my head reverberates inside my skull. The pain converges in my core and mutates into nausea. My body shudders as I lean onto one side and finally vomit. Every muscle in my abdomen contracts, squeezing me like a tube of toothpaste. I gag and gasp for air. My eyes burn as another shower of pale vomit spews onto the road.

I wipe my mouth on my flannel sleeve and spit. Puking up all that alcohol makes my stomach feel better, but now everything else is starting to throb. Somewhere, in another universe, I'm lying in bed next to Amelia, my girlfriend. Tomorrow we'd graduate and begin the rest of our lives. No more worrying about Rory getting in the way or Devon getting upset at me. It'd be perfect. Instead, I'm lying in the street, throwing up, while she texts Rory about what a fuck up I am.

Maybe he'll go over and comfort her while I lie here like a heap of trash. I had one thing. She held me together, and now she's gone.

My body throbs in time with my venomous thoughts, finally bursting the dam behind my eyes. Hot tears run down my face as a violent sob wracks my body. Each sputter sends fresh pain through me as I watch the mound of vomit flow toward the storm drain. I wipe my nose on my damp sleeve. I couldn't even make it home before breaking down.

What a fucking mess I am. A piss drunk, soaking wet, sniveling mess. Amelia would be disgusted. I am disgusted. I should just lay here and wait for some truck or bus to fix this whole ordeal!

As soon as that thought cleaves through my mind, the fear of dying alone in the dark propels my body up to standing. It seems to move autonomously, limping me out of the street, ignoring my brain's insidious pleas to stay. Nothing feels broken, thankfully. My hands burn, my shoulder is fucking killing me, my knee's stiff as hell, and my head is throbbing, but nothing is broken.

I can't do it. I'm too afraid. I have to keep going.

I pull my phone out, hoping it didn't get any more damaged by the impact or the rain. The cracked screen lights up, and my head jerks back to avoid the brightness. My stomach roils from the sudden movement. Twelve-forty. I was in the street for maybe fifteen minutes.

Jesus Christ. Fifteen minutes, passed out, in dark clothes, in the street. I could've... I should be...

My stomach lurches. I grab hold of the chain-link fence next to me so I can hold myself up as another torrent of vomit erupts from me. Fresh tears run warm tracks down my face. Hopefully, the rain washes that away before somebody's pet finds it. I wipe my mouth and keep moving, feeling soberer now that I've expelled ninety percent of the night's beverages.

I limp up the front steps and fight my keys into the lock. I head down the hall and flick the light on in the bathroom. Rummaging around in the medicine cabinet, I find a bottle of isopropyl alcohol. I sit on the toilet and kick my water-logged shoes off. Everything is gross and wet: pants, shirts, underwear, even the wadded-up socks in my pocket. I take my flannel off and look it over. The shoulder is ripped pretty bad.

That's what I get for wearing my favorite one out. I'm sure Amelia can... Right.

I strip down and hang everything over the shower rod before examining my injuries. My knee is already turning purple, and I have a long, bloody scrape down the side of my right leg. I swing it into the tub and unscrew the bottle cap. With a deep breath, I pour the clear liquid down my leg. My body tightens as the wound feels like it's been lit on fire. I suck in a breath through my teeth.

This wouldn't be as bad if I were still drunk.

I rip a long strip of toilet paper and pat the scrape down. Blood and alcohol run down the bathtub drain. I toss the TP in the bin and grab a fresh strip. I pour some isopropyl on it, then press it against my shoulder. My fist clenches tight as white-hot pain shoots deep into the muscle before subsiding after a few more pats. I start to pour some on my hand, but I'm shaking too much to keep the bottle steady. I set it down and wash my hands in the sink. It still burns, but not as bad.

I rinse my mouth out before meeting my own gaze in the mirror. My eyes look sunken in, all dark and red from crying. I am exhausted. Deeply, profoundly exhausted. There isn't enough sleep in the world to make me feel okay again. And I have to go on a road trip in two days. It's too late to back out now. I can't afford to lose the money I spent on that plane ticket, and I really need that car. Besides, what's left for me here? Amelia's gone. Devon will be gone. Jess will probably tell her friends about me dipping on her, and they'll think I'm a shithead.

They'd be right. I am a shithead.

My brain's too fried to run all the computations on how much tonight has sucked. I shut the bathroom light off and stumble into my bedroom.

I pull on my white T-shirt and sweats from earlier, so if I bleed while I'm sleeping, I won't ruin my bedsheets. I fall into bed and stare up at the ceiling.

Should I talk to Devon about this? Where would I even begin? Would he even care? At this point, he'd probably just feel vindicated and rub it in.

I close my eyes, eager for this awful moment to pass but fearful of the one to come. My aching body relaxes for the first time since Amelia and I left the house, but something still bugs me. I open one eye and look at my satchel hanging on its wall hook. I can feel Amelia's journal staring at me through the leather.

I get up and take it out, turning it over in my hands. It feels heavy now, much heavier than it should be.

What the hell do I do with this?

I open it and flip through the thick, brown pages. Each one empty, like me.

Maybe I should just throw it away. An empty journal already spoiled.

I flip it shut. The ship's wheel glints in the light.

No, I'll keep it. I'll write in it just like we planned, just like I promised.

I lie back down, holding the journal to my chest. It's all I have left now. I curl up around it like a dragon around his hoard. Visions of the open road flicker in my mind as sleep finds me at last.

SEVEN

"Pack light." That's what Devon told me months ago as we were planning this trip. Tank tops, T-shirts, shorts, ankle socks, the whole thing. I've always been a long pants, long socks kind of guy, so I threw together all six pairs of shorts in with a bunch of T-shirts and tank tops I scraped off my floor, thinking I'd be good to go. But nothing could've prepared me for the Arizona heat.

On the East Coast, when the wind blows, it's cool and refreshing. But when the wind blows in Arizona? It finishes cooking whatever's facing away from the sun. I will never understand what compelled some jackass to wander into the Sonoran Desert and decide all it was missing was a fucking city.

At least the flight over was nice. I've always liked flying. Being shoved into my seat by invisible hands as the plane shoots down the runway before that moment of weightlessness. That rush of leaving the whole world behind for a few hours in a tech-savvy soup can, only to wind up somewhere fresh and new.

I should've been a pilot. I'd probably be making more than I would at my upcoming job.

I tried writing in Amelia's journal. I thought I'd get down some happy memories of the two of us, but the only thing I managed to get down was myself. Each memory feels like a shard of glass being swallowed.

Amelia used to love reading my work. She was the one who pushed me to pursue writing for a living. Most of my writing assignments pulled double duty as treats for Amelia. Short stories for her to read before bed; poetry to leaf through in class; she even liked the terrible first draft of a one-woman show I wrote her as a Christmas present. And now I can't seem to get down a single letter without feeling my soul burn.

We haven't talked since that night, obviously, and it's been eating at me. We used to talk constantly. Then Rory came in and slowed that down, but at least we could still see each other. But this cold-turkey cutoff? My neck hurts from the emotional whiplash, or maybe it's from eating shit in the street.

I've been looking for an excuse to reach out since, so I texted her before the plane took off.

Heading to AZ. Wish me luck.

Devon's going to pick me up from the airport. I'm nervous to see how awkward things will be since our last real interaction was me throwing a shot glass at him. Besides, I doubt I'll be much fun anyway.

Checking my phone after landing reveals Amelia has not texted me back. This *completely* expected outcome makes me sink into my seat, still somehow managing to make me feel both surprised and like shit. My stomach's been in knots since I texted her five hours ago, making my lunch of Coke and peanuts all the more filling. As we shuffle off the plane, I get my first taste of the infamous

Arizona heat. Stepping from the plane to the jet bridge, I pass through a paper-thin curtain of scalding air. Instantly, sweat beads in my pits.

This is going to be so much fun.

I wander through the terminal, stopping at a little bodega to buy a lighter and a fresh pack of cigarettes for twenty-one dollars. I grunt a dejected sigh and swipe my card.

Gotta love getting scalped at the airport. Sky Harbor can bite my ass.

When Amelia got me into smoking, I promised myself I'd never buy my own pack, but here we are. Plus, I like the smell now. Reminds me of her. I tear into the pack and flip a lucky, something I've seen Amelia do countless times, before pulling one out and tucking it behind my ear. I toss the pack into my satchel, next to the journal, and take out my earbuds. I follow the signage through the snaking, bland halls of Phoenix Sky Harbor International Airport, much like I imagine a clump of shit might navigate the intestines.

I scroll through my music, looking for something angsty. I settle on Blink-182. The familiar opening to "Feeling This" starts, high school nostalgia washing over me as I continue toward baggage claim.

I step nice and close to conveyer seven, pleased most of the other passengers are still absent. I open Facebook and scroll through Amelia's page. She took down most of the photos of us, which is just the *coolest* thing ever, but seeing her face again is bittersweet. I think back to our screaming match in her front yard and cringe at the thought of that being our last conversation ever.

The conveyer belt whirs to life in front of me. I've always wanted to ride one of these things and explore the inner workings of a modern American airport.

Think of the amazing discoveries just waiting to be uncovered in the bowels of somewhere as fantastical as an international airport. Maybe I'd get caught by a TSA agent and be whisked away for an uncomfortable yet surprisingly intimate cavity search. Government employees are always such cold lovers.

The first few bags tumble out from behind the rubberized hanging flaps and begin their journey around the track. My eyes bounce from suitcase to suitcase, looking for my red, hard-shell one. The crowd of passengers grows around me as more luggage spills out. It's making me antsy, feeling them press in on me from behind. I bite my tongue and close my eyes, hoping the music will distract me from the growing mass of people.

Suddenly, I feel a tap on my arm. I dismiss it as someone bumping into me until another one comes. I open my eyes and look to my left, where I meet the gaze of a guy in a wheelchair. He's pointing at the conveyer belt and trying to tell me something. I pull one earbud to hear him.

"Can you grab that one for me?" He's pointing at a gaggle of black suitcases about five feet away and closing. I grab one of them and lift it a little, looking to him for approval. He shakes his head, and I drop the case. I grab the one next to it and do the same. This time he nods, so I pull it off the belt and set it next to him.

"There you go."

"Thank you. My wife just stepped into the bathroom. We thought we'd have more time before they'd start up."

Married? The guy looks about my age, maybe a little older, so twenty-four, twenty-five? What could compel a person to do something so stupid, so young?

I give him a curt "no problem" before turning back to look for my suitcase. I put my earbud back in to prevent him from striking up any further conversations. Maybe the five-hour flight and three-hour time difference has made me a *little* cranky.

I grunt as I pull my suitcase from the conveyer. Despite packing light, this stupid thing's half a big as I am. I extend the handle and start walking away, eager to get out of the crowd. Instead of smoothly rolling after me, though, the case drags along the tiles with a noticeable squeal.

United broke my fucking suitcase. Marvelous.

I spin the suitcase around so I can roll it on the other two wheels and pray the zipper holds. I head out into the oven to wait for Devon.

In the time it takes for me to toddle from the revolving door to the only lick of shade I can see, I think I might've already gotten sunburnt. I feel like a moth flying *into* a campfire. I hope my shoe soles don't weld themselves to the concrete. I only brought one pair.

I pull the cigarette out from behind my ear and light it, filling my lungs with sweet nicotine. Holding the smoke between my lips frees up my hands to text Devon.

Outside Terminal 4. Where are u?

I look up and down the airport street, looking for the bastard. Instead of Devon, I spot wheelchair guy getting into a taxi-van. A tall woman's standing next to him, black suitcase in hand. *That must be the wife.* She's facing away from me, so I can't see her face, but she is wearing a gray and blue tank top with some red shorts. He smiles at her as she pulls the door shut behind him.

It makes my heart hurt. I hock up a wad of phlegm and spit it onto the street. I swear to God, it fucking sizzles when it hits the asphalt.

Still nothing from Devon. I suck hard on the butt of my cigarette as a curl of smoke blows into my eye. I recoil instantly, rubbing at it furiously with the sweaty heel of my hand. When I look back, the taxi-van is gone, leaving me to boil alive alone. I look out past the looping roads and overpasses of the airport and see only beige dirt.

Sand, I guess? Nothing looks alive here. Maybe that's the point. It's a warning, unheeded by human hubris.

I can make out the Phoenix skyline a ways off through the heat distortion. All twelve tall buildings wobble like spaghetti in boiling water. "Phoenix is build out, not up," Devon told me once. Probably because the people here don't want to be any closer to the sun for fear of literally combusting. Everything looks like the after picture in an arson report, and I've definitely already inhaled at least a handful of sand or dust or whatever the ground is made of out here.

Is this what living on Mars would be like? Minus the venomous scorpions, spiders, and reptiles. Oh, and all the pointy foliage too. Mars is sounding pretty good right now.

Twenty minutes and two more cigarettes later, Devon pulls up in a bright red Mini-Cooper.

"Sorry!" he shouts to me out the window as I round the car and open the trunk. "My phone died, and I forgot the charger."

"S'all good." It takes me a couple tries to get my suitcase in a position that allows the trunk to latch. I hop in the passenger seat and buckle in, tossing my satchel bag on the floor. "This is nice."

"It's my dad's. He used to use it to get to work and such, but he doesn't drive it much anymore. So, it's ours to drive around town." He rubs his hands into the leather steering wheel.

"I meant the A/C, but the car is cool too."

We share a moment of silence, both unsure how to proceed. As the silence grows, so too does my fear of him bringing up the party.

Say something. Anything. Literally anything at all. Please, God, don't make me have this conversation right now.

"So, this isn't the car we're taking?" I finally ask.

"Nope. This one's just for today. We'll pick up the Nissan tomorrow at my parents' place. We're staying at my brother's house, by the way. It's just easier for them that way."

"How'd the old girl look?" I get an empty look from Devon. "The Nissan? How's it doing?"

"Oh! I haven't been over to see it. I'm sure she's good as ever. I haven't driven the thing since I came home for Christmas, but it was fine then." He gives me a small, reassuring smile.

"Wait, how did you get this car if you haven't been over to your parents'?"

"Mom dropped it off there for me and took a taxi back. I dunno, the woman works in mysterious ways." Devon shifts the car into drive and pulls away from the curb. "We've got to run a few errands before we head back home. I hope that's okay."

I have more questions about this car-swap thing but decide to keep them to myself. I don't know how old Devon's parents are, so maybe his Dad just doesn't like driving anymore.

"Yeah, that's fine."

"Do you wanna get food first, or are you good?"

I should eat some real food.

I check my phone one last time to see if Amelia has responded. Nothing.

"Yeah, I should eat."

"Cool, cool, cool..." His voice trails off, leaving us in silence as he merges onto the I-10. I want to put the radio on, play some music to fill the unbearable quiet, but I have no idea how the radio works. This is going to be a *blast*.

Our first stop comes into view as we turn left off one of the exit ramps: In-N-Out Burger. Devon has told me countless times now that I need to experience the glory that is In-N-Out. It's like a baptism, I think he said. I find us a table while he goes up to order for us without asking what I want. He just assures me there's a secret menu or something? I don't know.

I sit down in the booth and check my phone again. Still nothing.

Maybe she's still getting settled into her new apartment in the city. I think her program starts Monday? Yeah, she's just busy moving. That's all.

Devon sits down across from me with two of the largest burgers I have ever seen. I'm a die-hard Five Guys fan, but this monster burger might just take the cake. Devon must see the surprise on my face because he just smiles and sets to work devouring his own burger like a starved bear.

I take a moment to find the ideal spot to attack this beast of a burger. Finding a good spot, I take a bite.

Holy fuck. This thing slaps. Even feeling gross and jet-lagged, this thing fuckin' slaps. This is gonna ruin fast food for me.

"It's good, right?" Devon asks over his burger, which is already half gone.

"Yeah, really good." I take another bite. "This is like the first time you took me to Chipotle."

"Hopefully without the diarrhea." He gives me a wink.

"I wasn't expecting the salsa to be *that* spicy, okay?" We both share a laugh.

We're actually having a good time.

Devon finishes his burger in record time, leaving me to toss the trash once I finish mine.

"I'm gonna get some Animal Fries for the road, okay?"

"Some what now?"

"You'll see. Just go pitch the shit." He stands to get back in the six-person line.

"Gimme the keys. I'm gonna start the car then, get the A/C going." Devon tosses them to me. I bin the trash and head outside. Underneath the huge In-N-Out sign, I see my first real-life cactus. A bunch of them have grown out from the dusty ring of parched soil the huge sign is impaled into.

They look even pointier in person.

I take a couple pictures on my phone before hopping into the Mini and cranking the air. I unplug Devon's phone from my cord and plug in mine.

In-N-Out's definitely worth the hype, I type to Amelia.

If I can just get my foot in the door, just say the right thing, we can get this whole mess sorted out. I know we can.

Devon comes out a few minutes later, carrying a huge bag. My stomach growls in excited anticipation, eager for more.

We spend the majority of the day driving from place to place. First, we hit two different liquor stores to stock up for our stops before New Orleans. Then we hit a Dick's

Sporting Goods for two good coolers and a tent, and also so I could browse their fishing gear. We've also been to two other Walmarts, picking up various bits and bobs, snacks, and other goodies, but we've had no luck finding Zippo lighter fluid somehow.

"I promise, this'll be the last stop," Devon says as we pull into the parking lot of a third Walmart. "If we can't find any fluid here, we'll call it quits. Okay?"

I nod, and we hop out of our packed Mini. I can feel the weight of my exhaustion hanging off me like a lead plumb, but I push myself along behind Devon.

We walk up and down the outdoor aisles, slowly scanning each item.

"Scent Killer..." Devon mumbles to himself. I barely heard him over our footfalls on the linoleum tiles.

"What's Scent Killer?"

"You spray it on yourself so the deer don't smell you." He looks at me like I'm an idiot for not knowing that.

"And why, pray tell, will any deer be smelling us, Devon?"

"'Cause we're going hunting."

The only weapon we have with us is a two-inch knife and flint Devon got for his birthday ages ago. I'm not even sure if you can kill a whole-ass deer with a two-inch knife, but I am sure that neither one of us is sneaky enough to catch a deer with just a knife.

We stop at the end of the aisle.

"We didn't miss it, did we?" He turns and looks back up the aisle, scanning the shelves again.

"We've been up and down both outdoor lanes twice now. I haven't seen it."

"Fuck." He rubs at his brow, thinking of what to do next, I'm sure.

"We've got my little Bic from the airport. I mean, what are we really gonna need a Zippo for?"

"We don't *need* it, but I figured we could get some while we were out." He looks up and down the main way connecting all the other aisles. "I'm gonna see if I can find someone to help us. You mind walking through one more time?"

"I guess not." I round the corner to start back through as Devon wanders off. "If I'm not over here, I'm by the registers!" I shout after him. He throws a thumbs up over his shoulder.

As I wander back up the aisle, a thought occurs to me. I remember hearing somewhere that places like Walmart sell guns, whole-ass guns, in the southwest. My terminally northeastern brain just couldn't believe it, and so far, I haven't seen a single one.

I thought the southwest was all cowboys and guns and aliens, and I haven't seen any of them. Color me disappointed.

I am relieved to be away from Devon for a bit, though. We're getting along fine, but I can feel the question on his lips. Maybe he's worried about wrecking the good vibes we've got going. At this point, I wish he *would* just bring it up. The anticipation is driving me up the wall.

I scan each shelf again, checking through fishing rods, bait and tackle, hooks, line, and all that good stuff. Then the tents, small cans of propane, camp grills, and whatnot. I round the corner into the second aisle, determined to get this done with. I check each shelf, top to bottom, for Zippo fluid. Halfway down the aisle, I do find some Scent Killer next to the bottles of bug spray. And it's only fifteen bucks.

Maybe he knows a way we can use it to get high or something.

I grab the bottle and finish my walk down the aisle. I head over to the registers to wait for Devon there. The store is surprisingly busy for the late afternoon on a Saturday. They might be out now since it's past the heat of the day. Gotta plan for shit like that when you live in literal hellfire. I hop in a line so we can check out as soon as he gets to me.

I run through all the stuff we picked up today: Two coolers, one for lunch meats and road snacks, the other for drinks; a tent if we need to stop between locations for a proper, outstretched rest; an obscene amount of alcohol; a pillow and two blankets for the back seat; and a duffle bag for dirty laundry.

Is all this stuff gonna even fit in the Nissan? It'll have to be a tight squeeze.

By the time I get up to the cashier, Devon still hasn't turned up. I pay for the Scent Killer and take the bag from the cashier before sending Devon a text.

Did u trip or something?

Comin, he fires off immediately.

Sure enough, I can see the top of his head over the front-end displays, his mess of red hair bobbing up and down as he moves toward the registers. Instead of hopping in line, he slips through one of the unmanned lanes, empty-handed.

"No luck, huh?"

"Nope. We'll just stop somewhere tomorrow." He starts toward the exit, and I follow.

With the sun low in the sky, the desert look strangely calm, even if it's still way too hot. Then again, it might just be the residual heat radiating up from the blacktop of the parking lot. I pop the trunk and toss the bag in.

Devon gives me a funny look as I climb in the passenger seat.

"What's that look for?"

"Did you put something in the trunk?"

"Yeah, I got the Scent Killer you wanted." I buckle my seat belt as his look of confusion deeps.

"What are you talking about?"

"The Scent Killer! You said we needed some, so I found it and bought it."

"I did?" Devon scratches his chin. "Why do we need it?"

Am I having a stroke or something? He definitely said we needed to get some.

"So the deer don't smell us, Devon. I don't fuckin' know!" I throw my hands up in an exasperated shrug. I can't help but chuckle at how surreal this conversation is. "That's what you told me!"

I can almost hear the dial-up sound coming from Devon's head as he tries to figure out what the hell is going on. Suddenly, his face lifts, and he starts cackling like a maniac.

"Oh, oh, oh! I gotcha! Jared, I was makin' a joke. I saw the bottle on the shelf and just kinda read it as we walked by." He hits at the steering wheel with one hand and wipes at his eye with the other. "We don't actually need it."

My face turns red. I turn and stare out the windshield at nothing. I clench my jaw, feeling Devon's laugher punch holes through me.

Just fuckin' rub it, why don't you?

"Do you wanna run in and return it?" His voice trembles with barely contained laughter.

"Just take me home."

"You sure? We can—"

"I'm sweaty and tired, and I would like to be home now. Please." I try to hold my voice steady, but it warbles and creaks. Hopefully, he doesn't notice.

"All right, dude. Next stop's the house."

All this over a bottle of synthetic deer piss.

Devon backs out of the parking space and zips back onto the road.

Ninety percent of the jokes Devon and I fling at each other are basically just insults with a laugh track. We're no strangers to laughing at the other's misfortune or stupidity, and God help anyone who overhears us when we're on a roll, absolutely tearing into one another. But after the party, I'm having a hard time telling which of Devon's jokes are actually jokes or just ridicule. Trying to figure out what just happened makes our silent drive home all the more uncomfortable.

The sun dips just below the horizon as we pull into the driveway of a modestly sized ranch-style house. The red, terra-cotta shingled roof is a weird yet pleasing sight.

Devon's older brother and his wife are out on a cruise for the next few weeks, so the house is ours. Seems like a win-win to me; we stay out of Devon's parents' hair, and they stay out of ours.

We unload the day's haul, putting the perishable food and booze in the fridge. We'll go through it one more time in the morning and make sure we aren't forgetting any supplies. I make my way into the living room, eager to sit in something that doesn't move, while Devon goes into the kitchen to look for food.

"You want a drink?" he calls out while pulling open the fridge.

"I'll do a beer if there's some." My eyes wander around their living room. It's always strange being inside someone else's house when they aren't there, piecing together their lives from the various objects, furnishings, and pictures hung around.

Pictures of Devon's brother's family are arranged around some small potted cacti on the mantle above an immaculate fireplace.

They must get a lot of use out of it here.

Blown-up, high-res photos of bicycles hang with mirrors, giving the white walls some much-needed color and openness. Devon comes into the living room and hands me a Blue Moon before standing next to the photo that's caught my attention. A white bike, with leather seat and handles, leaning against a graffiti painting of a woman's head and shoulders in black and white. Waves of rainbow color explode from scalp-like hair. Her chin points up, but her eyes are looking down, exactly where the bike's sitting.

She looks beautiful. She looks like Amelia.

"I like this one too," Devon says, taking a sip of his own beer. "Brian shoots 'em all himself too."

I take a sip of my beer to wet my dry tongue. "He's got a good eye."

"They're all part of a set he's putting together. He likes finding weird or cool art and photographing it with whichever bike he's riding that day." Devon points over my head to another one: A red bike, black seat and handles, leaning against a white wall covered in red and black stars with a skeleton in a suit saying *No worries*. I roll the cold beer bottle between my palms as I scan the other photos.

"Is he gonna sell 'em or something?"

"Nah, he just likes doing it."

What good is doing something if nobody else gets to see it? That's like writing a story nobody'll ever read. Why bother?

"What're they called?"

"Sorry?" Devon crosses the room and sits in an armchair next to the fireplace.

"You said they're a set. Don't sets usually get titles or names or something?"

"Oh!" He takes a sip. "I think he called it *Lost But Seeking*, or something like that."

"Sounds a little cheesy, don't you think?" I take a long sip of beer, staring into the eyes of the black and white woman. The taste turns bitter and rancid in my mouth.

"He likes it."

Taut silence fills the room as I look for something else to say. I take another sip of beer and grimace. It tastes worse than the last sip. I gag it down.

"We got anything stronger than this? This ain't doing it for me." I set the bottle on the end table next to the couch.

Devon stands and walks back into the kitchen. "You want something in particular?"

"Whiskey, rum, vodka. Literally whatever."

I hear a cork pop and liquid pour into a glass. Devon comes back in with two fingers of brown liquor in a glass tumbler. I thank him as he passes it to me.

"You didn't have to give me this much. A shot would've been fine."

Devon settles back into his seat and looks at me with hard eyes. "Well, the last time I gave you a shot, you threw the glass at me. So..."

I bite down on my tongue, my heart suddenly hammering in my ears. I swirl my drink in its glass.

Is he making a joke? What am I supposed to say to that?

We stare at each other for a few seconds before I manage to string some words together.

"Look, man, I was having a bad night, and I was drunk. I wasn't thinking straight—"

Devon interrupts me with a wave of his hand. "Listen. What you did was pretty shitty, okay? Even if I did catch the glass before it broke. But I'll tell you what. I know I've done some shitty things after a good few drinks. Rough nights happen. Remember when I threw up on your bed that one time, sophomore year, and—"

"And you didn't tell me about it until I was about to go to bed? Yeah." I nod along as flashes of that horrific night spent cleaning up after Devon for almost two hours leave me on the verge of gagging.

"Right. So, I get it. Plus, even though you bailed on me at the start of the night, it was pretty rad that you came out after to hang with me. You really surprised me."

I shift uncomfortably. I hadn't expected him to remember this much from the party, but it seems to be playing to my favor.

"I really missed having those good times with you, and I think, besides the throwing glass at me part, it was a pretty good night. So, how about we set this shit aside and just try and have some fun before we gotta be *real* adults, yeah?"

It doesn't feel good, lying to Devon again, but he's right. My visions of the future, of adulthood, all gone. Amelia took them all with her when she slammed that door on me. In three tiny weeks, I'll be staring down into the abyss of an empty and terrifying future.

"Yeah, let's just... try and have a good time." I manage a weak smile before taking a big gulp of my drink.

Time for a change of subject before I blow this small mercy I've been handed.

"So, walk me through our route again."

I sit back, trying to relax as Devon lays out the trip. First stop, Los Angeles, California. We'll spend the first day there with his great aunt and uncle, and depending on how late we get in, we might do some sightseeing that day. The next day, Devon's planned a little surprise for me before we head across to Missouri to meet up with Riley and see Hannibal. We'll spend a few days there, then it's off to New Orleans. Drinks, museums, exploring the city, everything I've been waiting for since we started planning this trip last summer. One whole, glorious week. A fitting way to send off college life before the unimaginable drudgery waiting beyond. Then we'll scurry up the East Coast and be back in New York in time for me to start work with our new car.

"What time are we leaving tomorrow?" I ask, checking the time on my phone.

"Early." He hops up and sets his empty beer bottle in the bin. "So we should probably be heading toward bed."

I follow him into the kitchen and set my glass on the countertop.

"I'm still feeling the jet lag, so I think I'll have one or two more, then hit it." I grab the bottle of bourbon Devon poured from and refill my glass.

"All right, but I will drag your ass out of bed if I have to."

"Yeah, yeah, yeah, I get it. I'll be up." I take my glass and grab my smokes out of my satchel bag.

Outside, the sky is perfectly clear and unfathomably black. The light pollution from Phoenix proper makes it hard to see most of the stars, but I can still pick out a few: Polaris in Ursa Minor, Vega in Lyra, whatever the name of the top star in Cassiopeia is.

Amelia would know. She's the one who taught me the names of the stars, who got me interested in astronomy, in looking up at the sky.

I light my smoke and take a long drag. I scan the stars, constellation to constellation, looking for Orion's belt. Being in a totally different area of longitude and latitude makes it tricky, but soon enough, I spot the three kings, Alinitak, Alnilam, and Mintaka. Tracing up the left side of the Hunter, I settle my gaze on his shoulder, Betelgeuse.

Type M, red supergiant. Betelgeuse is the tenth brightest star in the sky, second brightest in Orion, after Rigel. It's Amelia's favorite star, in her favorite constellation.

I stare up at the Hunter with big, watery eyes. He stares back down with cosmic indifference. Part of me hopes she's staring up at him too, 2400 miles away, and wondering if I remember how much she loves the sky.

Amelia took me to this huge baseball field by her parents' house, about thirty minutes away from campus, so we could watch the stars. Neither of us had ever done it with another person, so we figured it'd be perfect. We drove over, hopped the fence, and laid out a blanket so we wouldn't get wet from the grass. We were out there for hours, just us and the stars rolling overhead. I never had a favorite star until that night, but I picked Rigel. It was as radiant as she was, I told her, and she laughed like I'd never heard before.

Like I'll never hear again.

I take a sip of bourbon and a drag on my cigarette. If I had a third hand, I'd be texting Amelia about this, about watching Orion, her favorite constellation, and hope she'd answer. I touch my scabbed-over shoulder, remembering the pain of that night. A pit opens in my stomach, sucking everything inside me into itself, leaving me empty and cold. My throat feels tight. My heart is trembling. I drop the cigarette and press it out with my foot. I finish my drink before turning to head back inside.

    I set my glass in the sink then go into the bathroom to get ready for bed. With my teeth brushed, I head into the guest bedroom off the hall from the living room. I strip to my underwear and lay on top of the sheets, hoping I manage to stay cool enough to fall asleep with the central air. I look out the window across the room at the night sky and wish Amelia were here to look with me.

EIGHT

Water rushes up my nose as I dive beneath the surface. The pool floor is slimy green with algae, like it hasn't been cleaned in ages. I kick, pushing myself back up through the surface, raining a monstrous splash on Amelia. She spins, half shocked, half giddy. She kicks toward me as I swim away from her, toward the steamed glass walls of the greenhouse. She shouts something I can't make out, but the joy has left her voice. I turn back to see her, ensnared by two large reptile men. The water in the pool becomes honey as I try to rush over and stop them from taking her away, but I can't. Before I even get close, they're out of the pool and dragging her down a busted open ventilation duct in the wall. I scream, but my voice is muffled and soft as I sink beneath the surface of the honey.

My first thought as my eyes flick open is how many lungfuls of honey are enough to drown a person. My bet's on one. I rub my eyes and sit up, already sweating as the dream fades.

I can't even get away from her in my fucked-up dreams.

I run a hand through my hair, shaping it into the good kind of bed head with whatever product is left in it from the day before. I pull a pair of shorts out of my suitcase and slip them on. I don't want to put a shirt on yet because I'll sweat through it before we get going.

Downstairs, Devon's sitting at the island, devouring a bagel like a snake would an ostrich egg. He's wearing a black Streetlight Manifesto T-shirt and gray linen shorts with a red and white baseball cap over his short red hair.

"'Ood 'ornin'," he says through a mouthful of bagel. "'Here's 'ore in 'hat 'ag."

"Devon, what the fuck are you trying to tell me?"

He swallows and points at the counter. "There's more bagels in that bag. I got up a little early and grabbed us some breakfast."

"Perks of having a car." I waddle to the bag and examine his haul.

Everything, sesame seed, onion, poppy seed... oh, yeah, that'll do it.

I grab one and cut it in half with the knife Devon left out. My stomach grumbles, but not the hungry kind of grumble. It's more the don't-you-dare-put-anything-in-me grumble. I take the first half and get two bites down before my stomach burbles again. This time, nausea follows.

All right, stomach, you win.

I drop the two halves on a plate and slide them in front of Devon. "All yours."

"You sure? I know poppy seed's your favorite."

"Yeah, I'm good. Gonna go shower." I head toward the bathroom, almost tripping over the two coolers sitting in front of the fridge. Devon lets out a giggle.

I take a few sips from the sink before climbing into a cool shower.

It's nine in the morning, and I'm already sweaty. Why do people live here?

I trade my red athletic shorts for some khaki cargo shorts I think I've had since high school and a red tank top. When I come out, Devon's finished both our breakfasts and is loading ice into the second cooler. I help put the perishables into the other one as he stashes water, soda, and beer in the first. We reload the Mini and hit the road.

Devon's parents live in a nice little suburb twenty minutes away from Brian's house. It's a pretty enough neighborhood. They even have some real, actual trees, with leaves and everything. It almost looks habitable. *Almost.*

Devon once told me about this old lady who was walking down the sidewalk one hot summer day. She tripped and fell into the road, which was thankfully empty, but got third-degree burns from the asphalt instantly. Pretty sure she even died in the hospital after.

I'm literally in Hell.

We pull into the driveway next to this absolute monster of a vehicle. This thing has to be three, almost four times the size of the Mini.

"Is that our ride?" The shock in my voice is a little too obvious. "I thought you said we were taking your Nissan."

"So did I." Devon lets out a heavy sigh, not too keen on hiding his dissatisfaction, either. We both stare, confused, at the behemoth alongside us.

"This thing looks like it *ate* your Nissan."

"Just... gimme two seconds. I'll figure it out." He undoes his seatbelt and goes around the car.

"Perfect. I gotta take a fat piss." I throw off my seatbelt and open the door, but Devon pushes it shut before I can get out.

"No. Just stay in the car."

All right, jeez. Chill out, man.

I redo my seatbelt and crank the A/C, watching Devon bound up the front steps and knock on the front door. I turn my attention back to the black monster next to me, trying to take my mind off my bladder.

The paint's scraped to shit, long white stripes running the entire length of the right side. Not to mention the wheels look almost completely bald and maybe a little flat. I can't see the interior sitting in the Mini because it's so damn short, but I doubt it'll save my resoundingly bad impression.

This Ford Expedition looks like the kind of car you'd get if you wished for one with a monkey's paw.

After a few minutes, Devon comes out of the house with two car keys on a carabiner. He's biting his fingers too. I haven't seen him do that in ages. The last time probably would've been finals last semester. He'd go into a test, cool as hell, come out chewing on his fingers, and looking like he just attended a funeral. I roll my window down a little to talk to him.

"What's the word?"

"So, my cousin totaled the Nissan about a week ago, and this," he points over the Mini at the Ford, "is the best she could do on short notice."

"Well, shit," I utter.

"Tell me about it."

We start unloading the Mini into our new ride.

"If we're quick, we can be on the road before the main heat of the day," Devon says, setting a cooler behind the passenger seat.

My dude, it's 101 degrees already. What the fuck are you talking about, the heat of the day? My balls feel like they're being soft-boiled.

The only upside is this car is much bigger than the Nissan, so we can actually make the back seat into a little loft with the coolers, blanket, and pillows. It actually looks kinda comfy.

Devon plucks a key off the carabiner and hands it to me. "You still good to drive the first leg?"

"Long as it starts, yeah." I take the key, looking it over. There are no buttons, or a fob, or anything. I slide the key into the door and twist it around until it clicks.

This car's gotta be older than me.

"You get set up. I'm gonna go say goodbye," Devon shouts over the cars.

I give him a wave and open the door. The front doesn't look too bad. Felt seats with a few dark stains, but nothing too crazy.

Dark stains are always better than white stains, especially in a car.

I climb in and notice the first big problem: the radio's busted. Of course, when I say busted, I mean *busted* out of the dashboard because there is no fucking radio. Just a giant hole full of capped wires where the radio should be!

I push the key into the ignition and turn it. The engine cranks a few times before turning over with a mighty, world-shaking roar. I'm shocked it actually started. I crank the A/C to max and buckle myself into our new death trap.

Arms full of extra water bottles and snacks, Devon knocks against the door with his elbow. I lean over and push it open for him. Immediately, I can tell something is off. His typical, high-energy boisterousness seems... diminished? Like his batteries have been drained by something.

"You all right, mate?"

"I'm fine." He buckles himself in, shifting to get comfortable. His voice sounds thin, but if he says he's fine, that's good enough for me. Devon likes to keep most of his personal shit to himself. Very much a need-to-know type situation. "Where the hell's the radio?"

"An excellent question." I slap the dashboard as he pinches the bridge of his nose between his thumb and middle finger.

"We'll make it work. We always have."

I slowly back out of the driveway, frantically checking every side to make sure I don't hit anything. It's going to take a long time for me to get used to driving this supersized shitbox. Once I've cleared the mailbox, I shift into drive, hold my breath, and ease my foot off the brake.

"What're we gonna call it?" Devon looks at me expectantly. "Every car needs a name."

"Like a real name or what?" I struggle to keep the car straight. The alignment must be fucked to hell because I constantly have to pull the steering wheel to the left or else we'll drift right off the road. I lay on the brake as we come up to the stop sign at the end of the road. The wheels let out a brief, shrill screech that startles both of us.

"That doesn't sound good." Devon rolls down his window and sticks his head out to look at the front wheel.

"It doesn't *feel* good, either. Driving this thing feels like trying to ride some hell-beast bareback with reins made of dental floss!"

Devon pulls his head in, a smile creeping across his face. "I like that. The Beast! How's that for a name?"

I lift the brake to pull through the intersection. The wheels give another short, ghastly wail as we pick up speed.

"It's fitting," I mutter.

After thirty minutes of cruising on the I-8, my body remembers how badly I need to piss. Devon updates the GPS on his phone to take us to the nearest gas station, which is about three miles away.

Since this is my first time driving west of Pennsylvania, Devon, our master navigator, decided we should take the scenic route to Los Angeles. Instead of taking the I-10, we're taking the I-8 down along the Mexican border. I'm not sure what scenery Devon is expecting me to enjoy, since it's all cacti and dust, but I put on a happy face for him.

We pull off the highway, bang a left at the exit ramp, and pull into the Sunoco parking lot. Devon explores the drink coolers while I book it toward the bathroom. With not a second to spare, I barely get my pants open before I piss myself.

After the longest piss of my life, I wash my hands and meet up with Devon in the aisles.

"See anything tasty?" My eyes dart between the many small bags of candy hanging on the shelf.

"You sure took your time. I was getting ready to come in after you." He elbows me in the gut and chuckles. I crack a smile at his stupid joke.

"I'm gonna step out for a smoke."

I walk past the gas pumps to the side of the lot where the Beast sits, baking in the sun. I was going to lean against it, but touching anything black after it's been in the sun seems like a bad plan. I retrieve a cigarette and put it in my mouth. I pat my pockets, looking for my lighter, and an unfamiliar voices pipes up behind me.

"Hey, man, can I bum a death stick?"

I turn to see some dude, probably in his late thirties, rocking a baggy white T-shirt and jean shorts. He runs a hand over his overgrown buzz cut and pleads at me with his eyes.

Amelia used to tell me about the comradery of smokers, about how you could ask anybody smoking for a cig and they'd probably give you one. It's like how Jeep owners wave to each other on the road. "It's just something you do," she told me. "'Cause one day, you'll be the one asking."

"You got a lighter? I can't find mine."

The man pulls a red Bic lighter out as I retrieve my smokes. I pass him one, and he passes me the lighter. With a thanks and a wave, the man walks away. I watch him go, waiting to see which car he gets into, but he just keeps walking straight off the lot and across the road.

Where the hell is he going? And where did he see my smokes from? These Arizonians are another breed.

Thoughts of Amelia linger on my mind. I take my phone out and find her contact. My finger hovers over the screen, hesitant. I know I shouldn't, but I really want to hear from her.

I need to hear from her.

I press down on the call button and put the phone to my ear. It rings and rings and rings, each time making me clench harder. I stare down at the lot in front of me, fixated on a few cracks in the concrete. The call goes to voicemail. Hearing Amelia's voice again makes my throat tighten up, but the beep sounds, and I have to speak.

"Hey, it's me. We, uhh... we're about to head out of Phoenix, and you're on my mind." I pause, not knowing what else to say but not ready to hang up. "We're having a blast, Devon and me. I'm sure you are too. We're heading to Cali today. So, that'll be cool." I look up and see Devon coming out, a few cans of Monster Energy in his hands. "I... I miss you. A lot." My voice breaks as I hang up the call and stuff the phone back in my pocket.

Why did I think that would be a good idea?

"Who you talking to?"

"Mom called me earlier, so I left her a voicemail getting back to her."

"Cool, cool. You want a Monster?"

I'm pretty sure a Monster would melt a hole straight through me, mouth to asshole.

"No, thanks. I'm good."

We climb into the Beast and get back on the road, with snippets of Amelia's recorded voice playing over and over in my head.

"In 269 miles, take exit seventeen onto Magnolia Ave," Devon's phone chirps.

It's gonna be a long, lonely drive.

After a few hours of cruising, we hit the Arizona-California border and a lot of traffic.

"What's going on here?" I ask Devon, who's spacing out while staring at the horizon out the window.

"There's a checkpoint ahead. Y'know, they ask if you have any contraband, we say no, and then we drive through." He shifts, trying to get more comfortable. With the coolers set up behind the front seats, we can't recline any further than a few inches. He pulls the brim of his baseball cap down over his eyes and crosses his arms.

"Do we have any contraband?"

"I mean, *technically*, you aren't supposed to transport liquor over state lines, but we'll be fine."

I ask a few more questions, but Devon just waves them off, saying I worry too much.

Somebody has to since you aren't.

The traffic moves slow, but we gradually make our way closer and closer. The bright yellow sign glares at us from about five cars away. *CALIFORNIA INSPECTION*, it reads in black, bold text. A couple of cops or guards or whatever patrol up and down between the inspection lanes.

One of them walks up to a car a few spaces ahead of us and knocks on the driver's window. He talks to whoever's inside for a minute before pointing off the side of the road, near the end of the checkpoint, with a few other guards standing around. The cop guard backs up as the car slowly drives out of the lane and up to the designated spot. The driver hops out and opens the trunk, pointing something as the cop guard looks around inside.

"Uh, Devon? They're checking cars."

"No, they aren't. I've driven this route plenty of times, and I've never seen them check out a car past just looking in the windows."

"Well, you might want to check again because they're scoping this dude's trunk."

That gets his attention. He flicks the brim of his hat and sits up to look.

"Oh, shit. Hold on, I gotta look something up." Devon takes his phone out of the cupholder as the car in front of us rolls into the inspection booth.

I want to look around and see if any of the other guards are nearby, but I don't want to look any more suspicious than I probably already do. Instead, I stare forward, watching the brake lights on the car in front of us turn off as he drives out of the booth.

"You'd better hurry up whatever you're looking for."

"I'm low on data, okay? Cut me some slack."

I shoot him an annoyed look before rolling my window down to talk to the cop guard in the booth. I make sure to give him a toothy smile as I greet him.

"Do you have any plants or unusual pets in the vehicle, sir?" he asks flatly without looking up from whatever is on the desk in front of him.

"Just the one sitting next to me!"

What the fuck am I thinking?

I look at Devon for approval, but he just shakes his head as I laugh a little too loud at my own piss-poor joke. The man looks up from his paperwork, clearly unamused, and my smile evaporates.

"No, nothing."

He makes a check on his paper.

"Do you have any alcohol or other substances in the vehicle, sir?"

Don't say anything stupid this time, Shithead.

"No, sir."

Another check.

"And you are aware that lying to a CDFA officer is a misdemeanor, punishable by a fine of up to ten thousand dollars?" The man's eyes flick between mine and the back windows, no doubt looking for anything suspect.

There is no fuckin' way that's true... is there? Hurry your ass up, Devon. I'm dying over here. Thank God I wore a tank top today: no sleeves to sweat through.

"Yes, sir, I'm aware," I say, as evenly as I can muster.

He looks the Beast over again, as if he could see straight through its metal body at the many bottles of alcohol stored in our cooler and suitcases, then stares hard at me.

"You boys have a good day then." He waves us through. I choke down a relieved cackle as my foot lands hard on the gas, speeding me into California for the first time ever.

"Thanks for the fuckin' backup there, bud."

Devon lets out a chuckle then reads aloud from the screen. "'A California resident or any other person may bring in a reasonable quantity of alcoholic beverages provided they are for personal use.' And that's on the state website, so we're fine." He drops his phone back into the cupholder and knocks his hat back down over his eyes. "Told you we'd be fine."

"Wish you'd said that *before* I perjured myself."

"Where's the fun in that? What's an adventure without a little crime?" He folds his hands together and puts them behind his head. I can plainly see the shit-eating grin spreading under the cap's brim.

"Go to sleep, Devon. You're a pain."

"Way ahead of you, partner." Devon jimmies his seat back another inch or two before settling into a comfy position.

The highway opens from two lanes to four, to eight, and somehow the traffic only gets worse as we go. The flat, barren desert finally gives way to hills the color of straw, dry-looking shrubs, and the occasional group of palm trees.

Devon's been drifting in and out of sleep for the last two hours or so, baseball cap still covering his face. His last bout of lucidity lasted only long enough for him to kick off his shoes and shift into the *comfortable* position of one leg on the dash, the other out the window resting on the side mirror.

I've turned the A/C off because the window's open and have resigned to drowning in my own sweat. While we were cruising, the breeze kept the interior feeling at least habitable, but now we're crawling at barely above twenty-five, and I am *roasting*.

I open my pack of cigarettes, now sitting in the cupholder unoccupied by Devon's phone. I've been chain-smoking since the scare at the border, and I'm already down to my lucky. I put the filter in my mouth and press the cigarette lighter in with a click.

The Beast provides but only to my own detriment.

"Do you have to keep smoking in here?" Devon's grumbling is barely audible over the wind and traffic sounds.

"Do you want me to pull over every time? We'd still be in Arizona." I crumple the empty pack and toss it on the floor by where Devon's feet *should* be. "And we should get gas soon. We're just under a quarter tank."

"Just add it to the GPS." He waves a lazy hand in the direction of my phone. His ran out of data, so we have to use mine for GPS until his cycle resets.

"I'm a little preoccupied here. Y'know, *driving*. Can't *you* just punch it in?"

With a groan, Devon pushes his hat back and snatches up the phone. He taps away on the screen. "There should be a Shell off the next exit."

"Are there any right along the highway? I don't feel like fighting my way back on from a proper exit."

"There's one close to Marie and Archie's. We'll just stop there if it'll be too much of a problem now." He tosses the phone into the cupholder with a loud crack, the metal base landing hard against the plastic bottom and the spare change the previous owner of the Beast left behind.

"Would you be careful with my phone, please?" I try to keep my mounting frustration out of my voice, but it's a struggle. Devon pulls his cap brim back down and settles back into place.

The traffic continues to worsen as we close in on exit seventeen. I'm not sure if the lanes are narrowing or if my brain is just playing tricks on me, but I feel like the space between the Beast and all the other cars is getting smaller and smaller.

Devon's snoring like a chainsaw being fucked by a motorcycle, and it's really starting to impede my focus. I'm white-knuckling the steering wheel, trying to keep the Beast from drifting into another car, which is plenty stressful on its own. Add Devon's cacophonous snoring, and my nerves are at an all-time high.

A spot on my right opens as a car merges into the further right lane. With my exit coming up, this is the perfect opportunity to begin thinking about contemplating how the fuck I'm going to get off the mess that is the highway around LA. I throw my blinker on and check my mirror. A few cars behind me merge left, and I see this sleek, red Mustang screaming into the newly opened space behind me.

Damn, Speed Racer, where's the fire? Good thing I'm getting out of his way. This guy would probably ride my bumper all the way to the house like a piece of shit.

I start speeding up to switch lanes when this fuckhead jumps into the right lane and shoots past us. I all but shit myself as I cut the wheel and narrowly avoid getting sideswiped. Thankfully, the car in front of me moved up, giving me about a car length to correct. I bite my tongue to avoid cussing the fucker out so as to not wake Devon up again.

The last thing I need right now is him chewing out my ass for almost getting into an accident that wouldn't have been my fault anyway.

Suddenly, the Mustang cuts back in front of me and lays on his brakes. My foot flies to the brake pedal and slams it into the floor before my brain's had time to understand what's happening. The distance between our cars closes alarmingly fast as my tires wail out like two cats fucking in a dumpster.

If the brakes lock up, I'm going to hit a car worth more than my fucking life.

The Beast screeches so loudly I think my head will explode as I shut my eyes and brace for the impact. But it doesn't come. We've stopped, inches away from the Mustang's bumper. The momentum rocks the car's whole body back and forth, straining the already worn suspension system. Devon almost rockets ass-first onto the floor, but his seatbelt holds him in place. Instead, he slides down, folding almost in half at the waist, as the chest strap snaps up over his face.

"Arghh! What the fuck?" He smacks the cap clean off his head as he goes from asleep to afraid for his life in no seconds flat.

"This piece of shit in front of us just cut me off! Damn near fuckin' killed us 'cause he laid right on his brakes!"

Devon pulls the seatbelt away from his face and pushes himself upright in the seat. "Could you please not kill us on the first fuckin' leg of our trip?"

Devon always gets this indignant, holier-than-thou tone whenever he gets scared, especially if he's done something embarrassing like, I dunno, slapping around at a seatbelt while screaming.

"How is this my fault? I'm the only reason you aren't eating your own asshole right now!"

He leans forward as if looking more engaged in this argument will make him more right. "Maybe a little situational awareness while you're driving in an unfamiliar place would—"

"Shut the fuck up!" I interrupt, swatting his words out of the air. "You've been asleep for the last few hours, and you have the balls to tell me *I* need to be more aware? Get the fuck outta here with that."

The sound of a car horn behind us pulls my attention back to the road. The traffic in our lane had moved up almost two full car lengths, and the people behind us were eager to crawl two inches closer to their destinations. Devon sits back in his seat as I inch the Beast forward.

We sit in silence as we continue crawling through traffic for several more minutes before Devon finally speaks.

"I'm sorry," he says curtly without looking at me.

"It's fine."

I want to say more, but I know it'll just prolong the fight and make everything worse, so I focus on the road instead.

As I pull off the highway, the silence between Devon and me provides ample time to psych myself out about meeting Marie and Archie. Devon's told me I'll like them, but I always get so quiet around strangers, especially important ones. Every mile I drive only makes the anxiety worse as it becomes clearer and clearer I actually have to meet these people. I would say Devon will have my back, but right now, I'm really not so sure.

After seven grueling hours, we pull into the driveway of a Craftsman-style house with tan siding and four white columns to hold the roof over the thin, full-length front patio. We park in front of a dark blue Lincoln, which I assume belongs to Devon's aunt and uncle.

I kick the door open and melt out onto the solid ground. Standing upright feels wrong after being cooped up for so long. I stretch tall and yawn big as several pops ring out from my spine.

I actually made it. I'm actually here, about to meet two strange people Devon's told me very little about except that we'll get along well. Three thousand miles away from home, away from Amelia, at a stranger's home. Why did I agree to this?

Devon claps a hand on my shoulder, and I jump.

"Come on. Let's head in." He leads me up to the front door, and suddenly I'm standing on the porch of Jess's house again with Amelia at my back. She's telling me everything will be fine.

I know better now.

I raise my hand to ring the doorbell, but I stop myself. One last, desperate attempt to avoid the inevitable. Devon reaches past me and knocks on the door.

"This'll be fun," he says, adjusting the bag on his shoulder. "I've told them all about you."

NINE

Devon's words reverberate around in my skull like a gunshot in an auditorium.

"I've told them all about you." Who tells people that like it's a good thing? People who like strangers...

An older man opens the door and introduces himself as Devon's Uncle Archie. He holds his hand out for me to shake, but I just stare at it, lost deep in my own head.

"He's a bit out of it from the drive," Devon says, pushing past me to give Archie a hug. "This is Jared, my roommate."

"Oh! So this is the Jared we've heard so much about!"

Please kill me. It would be so much easier. Like laying down in a road and... No.

"Well, come on then. Let's get you two out of the heat!" Archie leads us inside, asking questions about the drive and traffic and the like.

I leave the answers to Devon as I marvel at the beautiful, dark turquoise hallway we're walking through. The color reminds me of the water in Aruba when Mom took me for vacation. The water was so warm and so clear, I could see everything on the seafloor like I was flying above some mysterious, tranquil world. The walls are decked out with paintings of lighthouses and a cluster of fish-shaped mirrors I watch myself in as we walk past to the kitchen.

And the kitchen? The kitchen is even lovelier, with little bottles of multi-colored sea glass hanging from the ceiling in little nets and a lobster pot buoy with trawling line hung on the wall next to me. There's a white marble-topped island with a fruit bowl full of citrus and a key basket and matching white marble countertops. And over the sink is a huge storm window looking out over a small, fenced-in backyard. I cling to my satchel, feeling more at home among all the nautical memorabilia than I have in weeks. I take a step closer to the buoy, my eyes tracing the strands in the woven rope of the trawling line.

"That's genuine too," Devon calls out to me.

I turn to see he's made his way through the kitchen to the dining room, where he sits in one of six tall-backed, dark wood chairs around a matching rectangular table.

"It's true! And you'll never guess who helped us pick it out when we were up in Maine." His voice seems so much louder inside, like a gunshot in an auditorium. Leaned up against the counter, Uncle Archie almost looks like Santa Claus if he retired, shaved, and traded in his reindeer and sleigh for a fishing rod and sailboat.

"Was… it Devon?" Despite trying to keep it steady, my voice sounds all weird, even to me. I'm certain everyone else in the room knows as well.

"The very same!" He looks over at Devon. "You had to be… What? Eight? Nine years old?"

"I don't remember," Devon replies with a shrug.

"Marie!" Archie calls down a short hall branching off the kitchen. "How old was Devon when we went to Maine?"

After a few moments of silence, Archie shouts again, "Marie?"

"Give me a moment!" a voice calls back, soft yet strong.

A door shuts, followed by quick footsteps as Aunt Marie rounds the hall corner and comes into the kitchen. She's a small woman, probably a few inches shorter than me, dressed in a white shirt and pink button-down, a floral scarf, and simple blue jeans. Her white hair forms into short, tight curls that must take forever to do up. Despite looking a few years older than Archie, she radiates vitality. She leans against the door frame, thinking. "That would've been back in... oh-six, so nine years old."

Marie turns her attention to me. She's got this strange, wild spark in her eye, like she might do a backflip just to laugh at me when I faint from shock. It feels like she isn't just looking at me but inside me, probing around for something in my head. It reminds me of Amelia.

She moves across the kitchen with ease to shake my hand. "You must be Jared. It's a pleasure."

Her gaze is even more intense up close. It's uncomfortable to feel so *seen* by someone I've only just met, but I'm strangely transfixed and unable to pull away as my hand takes hers.

"The pleasure is all mine... Aunt Marie?"

"Just Marie is fine." She bats the formality away with a wrinkled, steady hand.

"The pleasure is mine, Marie."

She gives me a warm smile as she moves past me to greet Devon. He stands to embrace her in a long hug before Archie claps his hands to gather our attention.

"Now that everyone's here, let's talk dinner!"

"Always thinking with his stomach, this one," Marie says to me, making everyone in the room smile. I get the impression this joke gets told whenever new people come by for dinner. It makes me smile anyway.

"We weren't sure what you kids would want, so we figured the both of you could come to the store with me, and we could put something together! How's that sound?"

My stomach grumbles at the thought of a real meal. Aside from half a sandwich on the road and those two bites of bagel, I haven't eaten a proper meal today.

"Actually," Devon pipes up suddenly, "I think Jared'll probably wanna stay here."

Archie slaps his forehead. "You did all the driving! Completely slipped my mind. I doubt you'd want to spend another minute in a car today."

"Well, he can stay here and keep me company while you boys go to the store," Marie chimes in, to which everyone else agrees.

Hold the fuck up. What just happened?

"No, really, I don't mind—"

"Nonsense!" Archie's booming voice stomps mine into the ground. "You've done enough today. We'll take care of dinner."

Marie gently ushers Devon into the kitchen. "You boys should get going soon; it's already past five. We don't want to be eating too late, do we?"

"No, ma'am!" Devon calls as Archie picks a keyring out of the basket on the island. He gives Marie a peck on the cheek as he moves past her to the front door.

"Don't chew his ear all the way off, darlin'." He smiles, laughing like a madman, as she swats at him.

"I'm gonna stop in the bathroom quick!" Devon calls after Archie. As he walks past me toward the hallway Marie emerged from, he shoots me a little smile.

"You're welcome," he whispers.

I just wanna punch him in the throat. He knows how anxious I get around new people.

"Thanks," I mumble back, but he's already rounded the corner and disappeared.

Is he punishing me? I thought we already settled this. Maybe he's just butthurt 'cause he was wrong.

"Jared?" Archie shouts from the front door. "Is your car parked in the driveway?"

"Yeah, that's us."

"I'll have Devon move it when he gets out. That's quite a car."

Don't even get me started.

"Thank you. It's... all ours." I force a smile on my face in the hope it makes me sound happier about it.

"You guys aren't going anywhere else tonight, are you?"

"I hope not."

"Then you guys can just park in the back, and I'll park in front. Marie and I are going out for breakfast tomorrow, so you'll be able to get out. Devon told us he's got a surprise for you tomorrow." He winks at me and laughs that booming laugh.

I'd almost forgotten I had to be worried about that. Thanks, Archie.

"All right, let's roll!" Devon exclaims as he comes jogging into the kitchen.

The two of them head out the front, leaving Marie and me standing the kitchen in the most painful silence I've ever experienced.

Well, second most painful.

"Would you like to sit?" Marie fixes her paralyzing gaze on me yet again.

"I'm okay." I look around again, at the decorations, out the window, down the hall, pretty much anywhere that isn't directly at her.

"Don't be silly. You can't be standing around in the same spot all night. Come on."

She leads me past the dining room table into an unseen living room. The two rooms are actually one larger room, split down the middle by a wide arch along the ceiling. The living room walls are sea green and decorated with more lighthouse paintings and some old, framed photographs. A large rug covers most of the hardwood floor in the living room. A beige couch sits against the far wall in front of a three-paned bay window with two beige recliners flanking either side, all of which surrounds a glass-top, wicker coffee table. A large book with the unmistakable yellow banner and Playbill logo sits atop it.

"Sit anywhere you like. Would you like anything to drink?"

I make my way over to the couch and notice a short hallway connecting this room to the front door on my left.

"What do you have?" As I sit, Marie darts back into the kitchen and opens the fridge.

"We have water, OJ, milk, an open bottle of white zinfandel, I think, and... that's it."

"A glass of wine might be nice." I look to the paintings and pictures on the wall, absent-mindedly scanning over them. "If you don't mind," I add, for good measure.

A cabinet opens, and I hear two glasses clink on the countertop.

"Not at all! Think I'll have some myself as well."

She returns from the kitchen and hands me a stemmed wine glass, half full of straw-colored wine, before sitting in the recliner to my right. Her movements are so graceful, like she's floating just above the ground. Quite the difference from the lumbering Archie. His voice and stature might draw attention, but Marie's quiet, intense strength commands it.

My hand shakes a little as I raise the glass to my mouth and sip deeply. It's dry and mellow, with notes of citrus fruit and grass. "It's delightful."

"I'm glad you like it." She takes a sip then sets the glass down on a weaved rope coaster on the coffee table. "It's a little sweet for me, but I like the grassiness."

I spin the glass in small circles, watching the liquid swirl around the elegant slope.

Now what?

"You have a lovely home. I love all the... ocean stuff."

Ocean stuff? Christ on a bike.

"Thank you. We've got a collection of it now." She looks around the room with confidence and expertise, knowing the story behind each and every bit of decoration. "Not all of it makes it up on the walls, though. Did Devon tell you we used to live on a sailboat?"

I lean forward, interest piqued. "Did you really?"

"Absolutely, and we loved it. It was a big one, mind you. A decent-sized ketch, so we had plenty of room below deck, but yes, fifteen whole years on that boat. *The Lady Gray.* Archie named it after his favorite role of mine. Devon tells me you do a lot of writing. Do you know...?"

She asks me something, but I don't hear it because I'm no longer sitting on a beige couch in Los Angeles. I'm fishing off the bow of my own sailboat. I'm strong and tan, holding the fishing rod in one hand and a beer in the other. Amelia's proofreading one of my books in the chair she's brought up from below deck. Both of us enjoy the warmth as twilight settles over the water. I catch a huge fluke, and we cook it up for dinner. After we clean, we roll up the headsail and lay out a blanket to watch the stars. And we can see everything since there's no light pollution. Just her stars above meeting my ocean below. It's perfect.

"Jared? Are you all right?" Marie's voice cuts through my daydream. I blink a few times as it dissolves, and I'm back in the living room.

"I'm sorry?"

"Dear, you're crying."

I touch my cheek and pull back wet fingers. "Oh. I'm sorry. I didn't realize...." My voice trails off because Marie's staring at me like she's reading a page in a book.

She sees it. The mess, the anguish, the fear, all of it, plain as day. She's been looking at it this whole time, but now she sees it.

Instantly, I choke up. Her gaze softens with unspoken understanding, shattering the fragile patches on my already ruined dam. More tears stream down my face as the night of the party comes spilling out of me. All of it.

I can't decide where to look as I talk, so I just stare off into space, only occasionally glancing at Marie. Her face is indecipherable as she listens. I struggle to keep my voice coherent through the snot and tears, so she gets up to grab a tissue box off the dining room table for me. I use them liberally. By the time I've finished rambling, there's a pile of nasty tissues the size of my head sitting on the coffee table.

Marie stares at me, silent. I can feel her gaze pushing into my head as I continue avoiding eye contact. The silence is maddening. I can feel it gnawing away at me: her judgment, her revulsion. It reignites a tiny flame in my chest.

Just fuckin' say something already. Get it out.

"Are you still trying to talk to her?" she finally asks.

"Of course. Every chance I get." I snatch another tissue from the box and blow my nose. The tears have stopped for now, but my nose refuses to relent. "She hasn't answered yet, but at least she knows I'm thinkin' about her."

Marie lets out a sigh and picks up her wine glass. "I'd like to show you something."

She stands from her chair and walks over to a cluster of framed pictures on the wall. I follow but keep a few steps' distance between us. She plucks one frame off the wall and hands it to me. It's a group picture of twenty-ish people standing in a huddle on a stage.

"That's the cast photo from a production of *Cabaret* I was in a long time ago." She points to a young-looking woman, right in front, who's holding a man in her arms like Shaggy would Scooby Doo. His face is all done up in almost clownish makeup, and he's wearing suspenders with no shirt. "I played Sally Bowels, and the fella I'm carrying was my fiancé at the time, Monty. He played the Emcee. At that point, we'd been engaged a little over a year."

I nod as she takes the photo back and hangs it up again.

Seems a little weird to keep a picture of your ex-fiancé around the house, but whatever. Amelia kept up photos of her ex too. Is this something normal people just do? That shit's too sad for me.

"I'm sorry, I'm confused. What's this got to do with me?"

"I'm glad you asked." She crosses me and sits back in her recliner, cueing me to sit back down as well. "That photo was taken closing night. A week later, Monty and I would split up. He'd been seeing one of the other Kit-Kat girls behind my back. Just fell in love, like that. They moved out east together shortly after. It was... devastating, to say the least." She pauses to take a sip of wine to wet her lips.

Now I feel like the one who's prying.

"I wrote him letters, since there were no cell phones and long-distance calls were expensive back then. Since I had no address, I couldn't send them, either. So I had this pile of... oh, it had to be thirty or forty letter, all just lying around. After a while, I started feeling like my old self. I did a few more productions, redecorated the house, hung up new art, that sort of thing, and I put all the letters in a box in the back of my closet. I'd go through them occasionally when I thought of him."

Marie clears her throat and shifts forward to set her glass back on the coaster. "A few years later, I got a letter from him. He was lucky I hadn't moved. He wrote about how his relationship with Kathy, the other woman, had fallen apart, how he'd gotten kicked out, and how he'd been such a fool. All the things you'd expect from that kind of letter. But as I was reading the letter, I wasn't angry, vindicated, or happy even. I felt bad for him. That poor fool of a man, chasing love was the ruin of him. Me, I had new friends, new hobbies, new romantic prospects, but he fell back on an old flame. After that, I burned that letter and all the other ones I'd written. I didn't need them anymore."

I let a moment of silence hang between us to make sure she'd finished her story.

"So, why do you keep that photo up then?"

"To remind myself there's more to life than the people you fall in love with."

"Right... but, I mean, isn't finding someone to love sorta the goal? Y'know, find another person, get a mortgage, go on adventures. Isn't that what life is?"

"If you make finding love the most important thing in your life, you'll be alone, Jared. It's not something you can force, and it's not something to wait around all day for."

"Marie, I don't... I understand what you're telling me, but I'm not understanding why."

She gives me an incredulous look. "Really? Okay..." She rubs at her chin as her gaze drifts off mine into the space around us. "Have you read *Of Mice and Men*?"

"Of course, I have."

"Great. So you remember Lennie, right?"

"Yeah, big guy, mentally ill. Strangles that lady."

"Right. And Amelia. She wants space, but you keep reaching out to her, so she's Curley's wife." Marie gets this look like this literary metaphor is supposed to crack the code for me, but I'm getting bogged down in the layers of narrative. Frustration nips at my thoughts.

"So, I'm... what? Too nice? Too dumb to see what's happening? What?" I clench my jaw as that look of disbelief appears again.

"Amelia's asking you to stop mussing up her hair, and by reaching out and bothering her, you're just making it worse, like Lennie did. If you keep hanging onto her as she pulls away, you're going to destroy your relationship."

"But if I don't keep hanging on, she's gonna go off with this other guy!" My voice is catching in my throat. This is getting me way too worked up. " I have to keep trying, keep pushing—"

"It's too late for that, Jared. Can you not see that? Whatever's going to happen is going to happen at this point."

"Then what am I supposed to *do*?" I jump up from the couch, feeling fresh anger and upset blossom in my chest. "I'm supposed to just lie down and die? Roll over and let some other guy take her away? She was my future, we were gonna have a life together, and now all of that is fuckin' *gone!*"

Marie doesn't move a muscle as I gesticulate wildly. She just watches, harsh eyes drinking in the dramatics of my anguish.

"While I can understand this is a sensitive topic, I will not tolerate being yelled at in my own home." Her voice is hard and measured. It hits me like a bucket of ice water. I shrink back onto the couch as I realize how much of a shithead I'm being.

I'm yelling at elderly strangers now. Yeah, everything's just fine.

"I'm sorry," I say sheepishly. "I don't know what got into me." I eye my empty wine glass, wishing it were full again.

"I'll say this, then we can drop it: If you give her space, it'll do you both a world of good. If you keep hanging on, she'll out-grow you." She picks up the empty wine glasses and heads into the dining room. "That's my two cents. I do think it'd be good for you to talk to someone about this, though."

"I used to talk with her about shit like this. Sorry, *stuff* like this." I don't need to give Marie any more reasons to think I'm a bastard.

"You could talk to Devon. You two are obviously very close. I'm sure he'd be happy to offer his advice." She moves around the dining room table and walks into the kitchen, setting the glasses in the sink.

Explaining why that's a terrible idea would probably get us into another screaming match, and I've already embarrassed myself enough today.

"Yeah, I guess I could try that," I lie. "I'm sorry, could you show me where your bathroom is? The wine's gone right through me."

"Down the hall in here, around the corner. It'll be the first door on your left." She turns the water on to rinse the glasses as I get up and walk there.

Stepping inside, I flick on the lights and lock the door behind me. I check the bruise on my shoulder in the mirror. The deep, bloody purples are slowly fading to greens and yellows. It still hurts to touch, though. I meet my own gaze in the mirror. I barely recognize the sad boy staring back at me with those heavy, empty eyes. I turn away from him and sit on the toilet without lifting the lid. I let out a sigh and bury my head in my hands.

Marie seems like a smart woman, but I don't think she understands where I'm coming from. And the idea of talking to Devon about all this is almost laughable. The last heart-to-heart we had was when I told him about my feelings for Amelia, and look how well that turned out.

I take out my phone and check for any messages. Still none. I open Facebook, finding a few new photos of Amelia out at a pub in the city. Rory's with her, of course. Hand on her back or on her waist, lurking behind her like a shadow. Seeing her face again makes my stomach tighten.

I hear the front door open as Archie's rich voice fills the house.

"We're back! We're doing steak tonight!"

I flush the toilet for effect and splash some water on my face.

Just gotta eat dinner and go to bed. I can do this.

As I come out into the kitchen, Devon sets a bag of groceries on the island and walks up to me.

"I just put your suitcase downstairs in the guest room, if you need anything. How was hangin' with Marie? She's pretty rad, isn't she?"

"Yeah. She's something, all right." I move out of Devon's way and help unload groceries.

My plate is piled high with mashed potatoes, asparagus, and a beautifully grilled New York strip. Devon and I sit next to each other, across from Archie and Marie respectively. Devon is vacuuming down his food, as expected.

"God, this is so good," he moans between mouthfuls, making Archie and Marie both laugh. She shoots me a sidelong glance every so often, but she and I don't have anything more to say to one another right now.

"How're you liking it, Jared?" Archie asks me as he looks on with expectant eyes. Marie doesn't meet my gaze, opting instead to make a face at Devon.

I spear a few pieces of asparagus on my fork. It smells amazing. I work the long stalks into my mouth carefully, and they're amazing. Nothing beats the simple things; a little salt, pepper, and butter could make dogshit taste good, I swear. As the first bite clears my mouth, my appetite fully awakens, and I dive into the mashed potatoes with vigor.

And the steak—holy shit. Perfectly tender, practically melts in your mouth. The flavor is perfect, well-seasoned with thyme butter and just the right amount of char.

"This might be one of the best meals I've ever had," I tell him. "I can see where Devon gets his culinary skills from." They all laugh at that. Even Marie breaks a small smile.

"He used to be so helpful in the kitchen when we'd visit Phoenix," Archie says. "Always looking for something to stir or sprinkle, and especially taste!"

"Do you remember that time you let me get drunk off the cooking wine when I was eight?" Devon asks him.

"You did *what?*" Marie blurts out, swatting at Archie.

"He wanted to taste what we were using! It's not my fault he liked it so much that he poured himself a glass." Another round of raucous laughter erupts around me, and this time, I join in.

My phone buzzes in my pocket. I excuse myself from the table and step into the bathroom to check it.

It's a message from Amelia. The phone almost slips out of my hand as I open it up.

Can you please stop?

The bathroom disappears, and suddenly I'm back on the front lawn, feeling the world crumble beneath me. My stomach instantly sours, and my appetite dissolves. My head swims with a million things, all too foul to focus on. My hands shake as I struggle to twist the doorknob to get out.

"I'm gonna go lie down," I croak to the group as I shuffle into the kitchen a few steps. "I'm not feeling very well." They all turn to look at me.

"Are you all right?" Archie asks, a concerned look quickly spreading across his face. I keep my eyes away from Marie's for fear they'll betray me again.

"I'll be all right. I think I just need to lie down."

"We'll put your plate in the fridge if you wake up peckish!" Archie calls after me as I make my way into the basement without another word.

The basement layout is similar to the suite Devon and I shared when we met. Two small bedrooms with a shared living room. I check each room, looking for where Devon set my suitcase down. My phone charger and satchel bag lie on the bed. I plug my phone in and throw the bag on the floor before face-planting onto the unfamiliar bed.

Is Marie right? Have I already lost? Am I now to just lie back and wait for the end, like a pedestrian who catches a stray bullet in the gut?

I stare at my phone, Amelia's message searing into my retinas. Even when I blink, the words are there, like ugly scars on the inside of my eyelids. All I can do is hope they don't follow me into sleep and Amelia stays out of my dreams.

TEN

I don't remember falling asleep last night, but the puddle of drool on my pillow makes for compelling evidence. I don't remember any dreams, though, so that's a plus.

I roll onto my back and sit up. I didn't even bother taking off yesterday's clothes. Just passed out in my sweaty khaki shorts, like an animal. I strip down and retrieve some fresh clothes from my suitcase.

I'm shaking it up today with some khaki shorts and a *blue* tank top.

Really turn some heads with this one, I will.

I leave the dirty clothes in a heap with the clean ones. I run my hands through my hair, making sure to really shape that bed-head look.

I trudge up the stairs into the kitchen. Archie, Marie, and Devon are all sitting around the dining room table, coffee cups in hand and empty plates in front of them.

"Morning, Jared," Marie chirps.

"Morning," I mumble, rubbing sleep out of my left eye with the heel of my hand.

"How're you feeling, kiddo?" Archie asks in his booming voice.

Even in the morning, the man is a loudspeaker. I don't know how Marie does it.

"Better. Much better." I'm not sure if I'm trying to convince them or myself.

"I hope you don't mind, but I turned your steak from last night into steak and eggs. I saved you some on the stove if you want. I know you're not much of a breakfast person," Devon says.

A little food might do me some good.

"I can put some on a plate for you," Marie says, pushing out from the table. "If you'd like."

"That would be lovely." I walk past her and sit next to Devon. Marie reaches across the table and sets a plate of food in front of me before handing over a fork and knife as well.

God, even the leftovers smell divine. Maybe this is why Devon eats like a coked-out shark. I would, too, if everything smelled and tasted this good.

I take a few slow bites to get my stomach ready for digestion. It's a process like opening a pool after winter, check the pH, throw in some Shock, vacuum the nasty shit off the floor. Like Devon said, I'm not really a breakfast guy, so it's usually pretty hit or miss if eating this early will make my stomach unhappy. Normally I just lay in bed for an hour, jerk off, then eat lunch.

"There should still be some coffee in the pot if he wants," Archie says over his shoulder to Marie. "I made sure to leave some."

"Oh, no, thank you," I reply with a yawn. "Coffee usually gives me the sh—"

"Shoot!" Devon interrupts, saving me from having to apologize for another choice expletive. "We gotta get going, or we're gonna be late." Devon's up and moving before I've processed what he's said.

"Wait, where are we... Oh yeah, the surprise." I remember now. It takes me a while to be functional after waking up.

"Archie, can you give me a hand getting the car loaded up so Jared can finish eating?"

Archie finishes his coffee before hopping up to follow Devon down into the basement. With no sign of intestinal distress in sight, I finish my plate.

"What should I do with my plate?"

"You can just set it in the sink. I'll wash them later." Marie pours the rest of the coffee into her cup as I get up and walk over to the sink. "And remember what we talked about. Talk to Devon, okay?"

Time to dodge that question.

With food in my stomach, my brain finally turns on, and a question pops up. "Weren't you and Archie going out for breakfast this morning?"

"After you went to bed early without eating much, Devon suggested it might be nice to do a little breakfast with the family instead of going out. And those are his words, by the way. Breakfast with the *family*."

Marie's really gonna beat this dead horse. This is why I shouldn't yell at strangers. It makes every interaction uncomfortable afterward. It was nice of Devon to suggest that, though.

"I'll be sure to thank him on the road."

"He cares about you, Jared, so you'd better." Her eyes narrow, reinforcing that it isn't just a joke.

"I will."

Archie and Devon pack the car, the former telling the latter he snuck a couple extra beers for us in the cooler for when we get to Missouri. It's Devon's turn to drive, so I hop in the passenger seat, where my satchel bag is already waiting for me. He takes my phone to set up the GPS, so it doesn't spoil the surprise.

Why does everybody have to surprise me? At this point, surprise is just synonymous with sudden, painful disappointment, and I really don't need any more of them.

Once the GPS is set, Devon turns the engine over. The Beast roars eagerly to life.

"So, are you gonna tell me where we're going? Or are you gonna drag this out?"

"Can't you just be excited? It's gonna be fun. I promise."

I vaguely remember someone else telling me that before everything went horribly, horribly wrong.

"Can you at least tell me how far away it is? I'd like to take a nap."

"It's about thirty minutes, give or take another ten to fifteen for traffic."

"That's fine. Wake me when we get there, okay?" I push the seat back as far as it'll go and shut my eyes.

I half-sleep for what feels like hours as Devon drives us to our mystery destination. Occasionally, my brain collects enough awareness to tell which way we're turning or whether or not we're moving, but the majority of the trip is spent in unconscious twilight.

The abrupt cut-out of the Beast's engine wakes me up immediately, signaling our arrival. My eyes creak open like two rusty door hinges to see Devon staring at me. He's grinning like a fool.

"Where are we?" I half-yawn, half-mutter.

"Okay, so I know how much you like astronomy," he starts, giddy with anticipation. "And I know being in New York isn't exactly the best place to see the stars, so

I figured we could go see the next best thing!" He tosses my phone onto my chest, startling me upright instantly. "The next show starts in ten minutes, so we gotta get moving!" He's out of the Beast before I can ask any follow-up questions, like "But where are we?" or "Why must you always be so excited in the morning?" Finally, a thought pierces the brain fog and exits my mouth as I clamber out of the Beast after him.

"How the hell are we gonna see stars at ten in the morning?"

The three domes of Griffith Observatory poke up into the cloudless sky like the inquisitive fingers of a child. Devon's leaning against the guard rail in front of the Beast, looking out into Griffith Park.

"Isn't it gorgeous?" he asks me. And after spending over twenty-four hours in the desert a day ago, it is. The grass and trees are a welcomed sight.

We weave our way through the other guests, stopping for only a moment to marvel at the statues in front of the art deco entry before making our way inside.

This is actually pretty fuckin' rad. Devon did a hell of a job with this.

I used to dream about places like this as a kid. I loved science. Chemistry, biology, astronomy, even some of the cooler parts of physics. I remember my dad bought me a gyroscope for my eighth birthday, and I remember because I brought it in to school the next day to show off, and it broke. I cried for days after until Dad bought me another one. I wonder if I still have it somewhere.

But my interest in science waned as I got older and busier. I didn't have as much time to read up on cool shit like the Higgs boson or Claytronics. Eventually, I just forgot about it altogether, getting too swept up in school and being a horny teenager to care. It never disappeared, though; not completely, anyway.

The place is already a swarming mess, especially for a Monday morning, which sets me on edge. But I swallow my nerves as we come up to the Foucault pendulum right inside. I look down into the pit and watch the massive brass ball swing toward us, just shy of the pit's diameter. On the other side, several little pegs are set up with some knocked over. The ball swings away from us and knocks over another little peg.

"It measures the Earth's rotation," I tell Devon in an excited whisper. "The pendulum is suspended, so it swings in a stable line, and the Earth rotates beneath it, and the pegs measure how far the Earth's rotated so far." I look up from the pit to meet Devon's eyes. My face must look hilarious because he immediately brightens up and laughs.

"Told you it'd be fun."

I look up and take in the wonderous place that is Griffith Observatory. Two hallways extend out from opposite ends of the pendulum on either side of us, leading to all kinds of scientific wonders. Across from us are the doors to the Samuel Oschin Planetarium. Reading the name makes Devon's words click in my head: "We're going to see a star show!"

He smiles big as I let out a cackle, no doubt startling some of the other people around us.

"I've never been inside a planetarium before, y'know," I tell him, barely able to contain myself.

"Neither have I, so it'll be an adventure!"

We make our way around the pendulum pit, and I peek down one of the side halls. Ancient-looking telescopes and miniature models of space rockets sitting in glass cases hold my attention until I hear the familiar crack of the arc off a Tesla coil behind me. I want to break off now and explore, but I can't if we want to catch the show.

We hop in line, buy our tickets, and shuffle inside after only a few minutes' wait. We sit down as the spacious room fills. Devon cracks a joke about how the ceiling looks like a cosmic tit. I tell him that he's the tit, and the lights go out before he can answer, leaving us all in total darkness. The celestial projector kicks on, and the ceiling illuminates with our tiny, familiar slice of the Milky Way.

"The night sky," booms the narrator, "is both beautiful and mysterious...."

I tune out the voice and lose myself in the cosmic expanse stretching out before me. It's like I'm there, floating around in the cold, silent vacuum of space.

Distant stars whizz past as I try to name as many constellations as I can before they disappear from view. First, the zodiacs: Leo, Ophiuchus, Libra, and Virgo jump out plainly enough. Then some of the more obscure ones: Vulpecula, Hydra, Hercules, and Aquila. The celestial bodies slow as one huge, red star fills my field of vision with its brilliance.

It's red, so an M-class star. Way too bright to be a red dwarf and much larger than a red giant, so it has to be a red supergiant. And I only know one common red supergiant...

"Betelgeuse," the narrator expounds, "also known as Alpha Orionis, is the left shoulder of the Orion constellation and one of the most well-known stars in the night sky. At an approximate age of...."

The narrator continues on, but I've stopped listening. Amelia's favorite star stares down on me like the tiny, frail thing I am. The crowded planetarium suddenly feels empty as a retinue of intrusive thoughts bear down on me, souring the joy I felt before into bitter envy.

It's only a matter of time before my special moments become Rory's. I wonder if Amelia's gone stargazing with him already. I wonder if she's taken him out to that huge field by her parents' home. I wonder if she's told him about her favorite star, about her favorite constellations. I wonder if they undressed each other in that quiet dark like we did, fucked like we did, held each other like we did that night. I wonder how long it will take for her to forget me, or rather, how long it took her to.

I can't get up and leave because if someone so much as looks at me right now, I'm afraid I'll dissolve. Instead, I cover my face with my hands to hide my anguish as the show continues, undisturbed, around me.

When the lights come up, I jump from my seat and race out of the planetarium. I push past a group of other tourists lined up for the next show and hurry into the bathroom near the pendulum. I lock myself in one of the stalls and clamp one hand over my mouth. A muffled sob chokes out of me as a tear drips from my cheek and lands on my shorts. I pinch my eyes shut, trying desperately to find some internal silence, but everything inside me is screaming like it's on fire.

I can't even enjoy the night sky anymore. How much more am I going to lose because of her?

My phone buzzes a few times. I pull it out with my free hand to see Devon calling me. My embarrassment and sadness sharpen into white-hot anger. My grip on my phone tightens until my whole arm is shaking.

He probably knows what happened. That's why he's doing this. He's trying to fill the void Amelia left. Like he could even hope to come close.

I shove my phone back into my pocket and wipe my face on my arm before unlocking the stall.

He's leaning up against the wall next to the bathroom, face buried in his phone, when I come out.

"I was just texting you," he says, looking up. "I called, but you didn't answer. You okay?"

"Fine. Just had to piss really bad." I hold my voice as steady as I can.

"Did you like the show? It's always so wild to get a glimpse of how big everything is out there."

"Yeah, really puts a lot of things in perspective."

"Exactly!" He tucks his phone back in his pocket. "So, which side do you wanna hit first? Tesla coil or telescopes?"

We make our way through the various exhibits, Devon hanging off me like a toddler. We read plaques, peruse displays, watch the Tesla coil zap a faraday cage, all the good stuff. I take some pictures of LA from the patio area while Devon explores on his own before making my way back to the pendulum to meet him. Two more pegs have been knocked over since we arrived. I look up at the ceiling around the pendulum and notice the mural surrounding it.

Somebody ought to call up Florence to make sure Michelangelo's body's still there because whoever painted this mural's got a huge hard-on for the guy. Looks like a bootleg Sistine Chapel mural, but shitty. Maybe next time the artist fucks his corpse, they should grab some talent before they finish.

Devon meets me, and we explore the gift shop so I can buy a star map before we head back out to the Beast. We pit-stop at Archie and Marie's to shower and cool off. After throwing on some fresh clothes and eating a quick lunch, I climb in the backseat to lay down. Devon starts the Beast, and we make our way toward our next stop: Missouri.

"People with kind hearts burn with the hottest anger," my dad told me that when I was ten while he and my mother were getting divorced. He moved into a two-bedroom apartment on the outskirts of town while Mom kept the house.

This one time, I was over at his place trying to do school work in the living room while he was talking to Mom on the phone in the kitchen. By that point, I had gotten used to them fighting. They did it pretty much constantly except for meals. The divorce, of course, only made things worse as the courts were handing out alimony and child support rulings. But the ugliest fights were always about me.

See, I learned to curse from my dad. He would always throw in a shit or a fuck for emphasis or just to make little Jared laugh until he peed himself. But it was the fights over spending time with me that taught me how to curse.

"Jeanine, you rat fuckin' bitch, you will not fuckin' keep me away from my own fuckin' kid! Do you hear me?" Dad smashed his phone down on the counter several times while screaming that last part over and over again until he threw it across the living room into a vase. That was the first time I'd ever pissed myself out of fear.

Instantly, I started screaming and sobbing like a baby. His anger melted away as he saw me weeping in a puddle of my own piss on the floor. But when he walked over to pick me up, I flinched away from him. This man, who had given me that gyroscope, who encouraged me to sing in the shower no matter how bad it was, who helped me with school projects even when he wasn't supposed to, had never hit me in my life, but in that moment, it didn't matter. That was when he started to cry too. He got down on one knee next to me and apologized through his own sobs. He picked me up, stripped me down, and set me in the bathtub. Of course, I could do this all by myself at ten, but I was too distraught to do much of anything.

Before he walked away to clean up the piss, I stopped him and asked, "Why do you get so angry at Mommy?"

"People with kind hearts burn with the hottest anger, Jared. And if you aren't careful, it'll burn y'away to nothing."

I think I'm a kind person when it counts, but right now, I've got nothing left to burn up. So what the hell?

We stopped for more cigarettes and gas before hopping on the highway. I fell asleep, napped for maybe an hour or two, but I can't be sure. Judging anything around LA by time spent traveling is an exercise in absurdity, because covering ten miles in two hours is not only common but expected. Looking out the window now, I can see the sky painted with rich oranges and pinks. No gray twilight signaling proper evening yet.

The current plan is for Devon to drive all night while I rest up, then I'll tap in for him so he can rest, then he'll finish the leg. All said and done, if we're speedy, we can do it in just under twenty-four hours.

My phone charger is plugged into the center console with my phone attached. It sits next to me, open. Still no new messages. Just that one.

Can you please stop?

My anger's gone. My despair? Gone. Everything burned away after the planetarium, leaving me with nothing but cold apathy.

I pull out my journal and pen from my satchel bag and search the skyline for inspiration. It's difficult to focus on anything with Devon singing along to some horrible country song, but I am determined to block him out. The heavy brown paper eyes my pen thirstily.

Write a poem about all the obnoxious shit Devon does, Catullus 16 style.

I start brainstorming some events to draw inspiration from.

That one time he microwaved a ceramic bowl of soup for five minutes and thought he could take it out with just his hand. We had to throw out the entire carpet and wipe down the wall after that one.

Or that time Devon drew a dick on my face after I passed out a party. "It's just ball-point pen!" he said, like I was supposed to be grateful he hadn't Sharpied a dick on my forehead.

Or when he threw up in my bed that one time.

Or when he...

I wave the gathering thoughts away. Besides, if I'm going to write something in the journal, it's gotta be something Amelia's going to want to read. Otherwise, why bother? I sigh and toss both things back in my bag and pull out my cigarettes. I reach forward and push the cigarette lighter in on the console, startling Devon. I hold the smoke up, so he knows what I'm doing. He rolls his eyes and returns his attention to the road.

When the lighter pops out, I grab it and press the red-hot metal to the end. Devon cracks the windows in the back as I kick my shoes off and stare at the passing hills along the I-15.

"Jared, you awake back there?" Devon says, tapping my foot.

I wonder how Devon could reach my foot from the driver's seat before jolting awake in a momentary panic only to realize we aren't moving anymore. Devon's standing in the open door by my feet. I can see the sun just behind him, just inches away from setting completely.

"I am now," I groan as I stretch.

"Come check this out. Side adventure!" He disappears from view, leaving me to scratch the sleep from my eyes and climb out after him.

The highway, if we're even still on it, has narrowed to one lane in each direction. We're pulled off onto the shoulder of the road, and we're back in the desert, surrounded by sand and death.

"Where are we?" I turn to ask Devon, but he's nowhere to be seen. I check behind me to make sure he hasn't climbed back into the car when I hear him call out from way off behind the Beast.

"Come on!"

I walk past the Beast and see him about thirty paces off the road, staring into the distance.

"Where are we?" I shout, cupping my hands around my mouth.

"Barely into Nevada! But look!" He lifts his arm to point at something. I follow his arm to what looks like a tall, orange rock mound.

"Why are we stopping to look at rocks?"

"Just come here!"

For fuck's sake.

A few drops of sweat are forming on my forehead because, even on the edge of night, this quadrant of the country is a fucking dumpster fire. I step off the road toward Devon, being careful to keep an eye out for any nocturnal stinging critters.

"What is it?" I demand as I come up next to him. Devon doesn't look at me. He keeps his head turned toward the rock mound. "What is so special about these damn—"

The words catch in my throat as I turn to look as well. The mound isn't actually a mound but a rock arch. Well, sort of a rock arch; the aperture is small and circular, about three-quarters of the way up from the ground, but I can see the last traces of burnt orange light on the gray sky behind it clear as crystal.

"Pretty cool, huh?" Devon says, nudging me with his elbow.

It is cool, but I'm not in the mood to give him a win right now.

"It's just rocks, dude. We have rocks in New York." I turn on my heel and start back toward the Beast. I wipe a small fleck of dust out of my eye as Devon deflates behind me.

I'm being a dick, and I'm gonna feel bad about it later, but right now, I don't care.

We silently pile back in and pull back onto the road.

The first twenty-four-hour gas station in Colorado is a welcome oasis from the bland drudgery that is Utah. It's about 2:00 a.m. according to my phone, and Devon's spent. He runs inside the station to piss while I pump some more gas into the Beast's thirsty maw.

As I twist the gas cap back into place, Devon comes bounding out with a one-pound bag of Sour Patch Kids.

"'His hwas the 'ast one 'hey had!" he tells me, his mouth full of sticky candy. He swallows the sugary mass and hands me the bag. "A little treat to keep you company while I sleep."

"Thanks," I mumble flatly. True to my own word, I'm starting to feel bad about being so rude, but I don't know how to apologize and mean it right now.

He hops in the back as I climb in the driver's seat, ready for round two.

Devon puts *Ed, Edd, and Eddy* on his phone to watch while he falls asleep. He'd downloaded them in case we got stuck somewhere with no service for a while.

I take my eyes off the road to flick through my own music, looking for anything to drown out the Eds' obnoxious chatter. In the faint moonlight, I can see the outline of the trees along the median. I wish I could see them better. I miss real plants.

As the hours and miles tick by, the sun finally pokes up over the horizon. For the first time in what feels like months, I lay eyes on coniferous trees.

Mercifully, Devon's phone died about two or three hours ago after *someone* unplugged the charger from the center console.

At least I can enjoy a few hours of not pretending to be all right. It's exhausting.

Without warning, the Beast's right front tire hits a massive pothole, wrenching my hands off the steering wheel. Everything inside shifts diagonally about a foot and a half before being shoved back into place a second later.

Devon's head hits the back door with a loud, bony thwack followed by a torrent of expletives. My foot slams on the brake as my hands scramble to regain control of the steering wheel. Thankfully, it's still early enough that only a few cars are on the road with me. Less targets to hit.

"What the fuck was that?" Devon yells, having been, once again, startled from asleep to what-is-trying-to-kill-me mode. "Did we hit something?" He rubs furiously at the back of his head.

With the steering wheel back in my hands, I speed back up to cruising. "It was just a pothole. Go back to sleep."

He grumbles something under his breath before rolling over and letting out a huff. I bite my tongue and try to focus on the road.

It doesn't take long for me to notice something's wrong with the Beast after hitting that pothole. I throw on my blinker to move into the center lane, to avoid any other extra-large potholes, and I notice the steering wheel feels stiff. I throw my blinker on again and move back into the right lane. Same thing.

"God damnit," I mutter to myself. "This cannot be good." I reach into the backseat and nudge Devon. He rolls over and grunts.

"I need you to look up an auto repair place near us."

"Why?" Devon pulls himself into a seated position and grabs his phone. "And why is my phone dead?"

Whoops.

I toss mine back to him.

"Something's up with the steering." I try shaking the wheel back and forth, hoping it'll loosen up, but it doesn't.

It's always gotta be something. God damnit!

"Mother fuckin' piece of shit!" I crack the steering with the heel of my hand.

"Get off at the next exit, then make a right. Once you hit Main, take another right. Paul's Auto Repair will be on the left side."

"Are they gonna be open?"

"Says they open at seven."

"Works for me."

I stick my hand back, palm up, for my phone.

"You're welcome," Devon says, dropping it into my hand.

Pulling into Paul's Auto Repair is as frustrating as it is difficult. Everything around here is fucking tiny. This town looks like it's still waiting for the railroad to come through. After ten minutes of brain-splitting aggravation, I manage to finagle the Beast in front of the garage. We hand the guy behind the desk one of our keys, and Devon sets to filling out the paperwork. I sit down in one of the small armchairs in the lounge area. The door into the garage is made of glass, and through it, I can see the Beast get hoisted up on one of those powerlifter things. I'm picking at a little bag of Cheez-Its I grabbed from a bowl on one of the tables. My leg bounces furiously.

Finally, a gruff, older-looking man comes around to the front desk. "You two are here with the Ford Expedition, right? Arizona plates?"

Devon jumps up. "Yeah, that's us. What's going on with it?"

"Well, the problem was pretty easy to find. You're pretty much out of power steering fluid." The man shuffles through some papers he brought in with him.

"But we had that checked just a few days ago in Arizona and it was fine. How can it be low?"

"Well, that brings me to the second part: There's a leak in your power steering pump. Now, that can happen for a number of reasons. It's pretty much always wear and tear, but—"

"How long will it take to fix?" I pipe up.

The man shrugs. "If we have another pump that we can put in, it'll take a few hours. But if not, it'll take a few days for another one to get here."

A few days? It's already Tuesday. We're supposed to be in New Orleans by Friday. We don't have a few days. I will not be fixing hotel reservations, museum tickets, or dinner reservations. Un-fucking-believable!

Without a word, I stand up with my satchel and head outside. I pull out my smokes and take out the lucky. Amelia used to say it's bad luck to smoke the lucky before the pack is finished.

I'm pretty sure my luck can't get any worse.

I fish around in my bag for a lighter.

"Hey, Jared!" Devon calls to me from the door. "Don't worry. We're gonna figure this out."

"Unless you have a lighter, go back inside."

"Come on, dude. This'll just be another adventure!"

I clench my fist, crushing the cigarette in my hand. I whip around to face him. "Can you stop *fucking* saying that?" The words hit him like a buckshot. "This is not an *adventure*, Devon, because you and I don't go on *adventures*. Amelia and I went on *adventures*. You and I don't go stargazing together. Amelia and I went stargazing."

I throw my mushed cigarette on the ground and stomp on it. "I don't know what you think aping my relationship with her will get you, but you need to cut it the fuck out!"

"What the fuck are you talking about, Jared?" Devon's face screws up in a look of disgusted confusion. "I've been trying to have fun with you, but you've been a piss ant since we left the observatory. What the hell is goin' on?"

"Don't play dumb, you fucker!" I close the distance between us, getting right up in his face. He stands his ground, looking me dead in the eye. He knows I won't hit him because he'd tie me in a knot.

"I don't know how you know what happened after the party. I don't know if you went through my phone or some shit while I was asleep. But I'll tell you what I do know: You will *never* be as important to me as she was. You got that? Ever!"

I'm so angry, my head feels like it's going to explode. At this point, I'm only seeing red, and I'm way past calming down. Devon stiffens up as my words land, like he's being electrocuted.

"I should've never come on this trip because it has cost me everything. So, I am going to find a coffee shop or somewhere with free Wi-Fi, I am going to book an Uber to the nearest airport, and I am going back to New York to *beg* Amelia to take me back."

I turn and storm out of the parking lot, leaving Devon standing there, stunned and slack-jawed.

ELEVEN

I stalk down Main Street like a panther ready to kill. My third cigarette is clamped between my lips. I found the lighter in the bottom of my satchel. At this rate, I'm gonna need a new pack before I get to the airport.

That was a really fucked up thing to do to him.

I look up and down the quaint town center. A barbershop, a tiny book store, a pharmacy, some pricy-looking clothing stores—fuck, they even have a little toy shop. All of them in old-looking brick and mortar buildings. Really hammers home that small-town vibe. But still no coffee shop. *There's got to be one somewhere.*

Besides the mechanics, I have yet to see a single local. I'm not sure it's because only three hundred people live here or if it's still too early for them. I look around again.

Do CVS's have Wi-Fi? That CVS might actually be a dispensary unless they've swapped the red cross out for a green one.

As I weigh the pros and cons of switching out caffeine for THC, I see her. That beautiful, copyrighted mermaid smiles coyly at me from down the street. For the first time ever, Starbucks saves the day. Their coffee sucks but is statically better than no coffee.

I throw open the door and discover where everybody's been hiding. The place is packed, wall to wall. There's not a single open seat, and the line is pretty much to the door.

I just cannot get away from these crowds, can I?

My anxiety transmutes into spite. This building could be packed like a Tokyo subway for all I care.

Fuckin' bring it on.

I stare at the menu, replaying the earlier conversation in my head. I feel bad for blowing my top at Devon, but there isn't much I can do now. Normally I'd just call Amelia when I get worked up, but since she wants nothing to do with me, I guess stewing in my own juices until I explode is how I'll be doing things now.

That's a dogshit way to be, and I know it.

I order a large—sorry, *venti*—iced coffee. A few eyes dig into my back. No doubt the locals are sizing up the not-so-fresh-faced stranger in their midst. I grew up in a small town too; I know how this game goes.

I pay for my drink and move to the pick-up counter. I futz with a straw because I know this is one of the stupidest things I've ever done, even if I'm not going to admit it.

Why does this keep happening to me? Why can't anything just work out?

A tap on the shoulder pulls me out of my thoughts. I turn around, half expecting to see Devon pulling back to sock me in the mouth. Instead, it's some blonde woman in a plain black T-shirt and comfy-looking jeans with a blue, green, and black plaid button-down tied around her waist. She doesn't have a coffee in her hands, so maybe she just wants to get at the counter.

"S'cuse me, I think your shirt's inside out. I'm sorry, but I'd want to know, so...."

I reach over my shoulder and find the tags hanging out like a pair of batwings. My face blooms lobster red as my anger implodes into humiliation.

"Venti iced coffee for Jared!" calls the barista. I open my mouth to say something, but nothing comes out. I just stand there like an idiot. "You Jared?" I nod, and he sets the drink down in front of me.

"Thanks," I squeak out. "And thanks for telling me." I pick up my coffee as she gives me a pity smile and walks back to the line.

Now I know why everybody was staring at me when I got to the counter.

"Do you guys have a bathroom here?" I ask the barista when he walks past again.

"It's out of order right now, but there's a car place up the road with one if you need it. I think it's the closest."

Of course, it is. Is there a "Kick Me" sign on my back or something?

I thank him again and rip the tags off my collar with my free hand. I look around for a spot to park my ass for a while, but in the fifteen minutes since I walked in, no one's moved. If anything, more people have come in to stand around at the countertops between the tall chairs. The ceiling starts closing in as more patrons move toward me from the order line. I hope they have some outside seating as I head toward the door.

Around the side of the building sit several circular tables, some with four chairs, others with only two. Toward the back of the makeshift patio is one, thankfully empty, table. I weave between the occupied ones, clutching my satchel bag close to keep it from hitting anyone. I take out my journal and pen before setting the bag in one chair and sitting in the other.

I eye the first page, rolling the heavy, chrome fountain pen in my hand. I don't know how to say what I need to, so I start plotting the words in my head.

"Dear Amelia..." *Do people still start letters like that? It sounds so dated.*

"Dearest Amelia, I hope this letter finds you in good health. It has been many months since my plow hath broke, and I am thusly forced to work the hardened soil by hand. Joshua and I fear the harvest will be much diminished on account of the slow, tedious pace."

I smile at the stupid joke before shaking it from my head.

"Hey, it's me..." *No.*

"How've you been doing?" *No, that's stupid. She can't answer. It's a letter, dumbass.*

Okay, fuck the greeting. I can go back and write that later.

The pen hovers over the paper as if they were two magnets repelling one another. I prop my head up with my other hand, kneading my forehead like bread dough.

I've got the fancy paper; I've got the nice pen; now I just need to write some fuckin' words so I can get back to—

"S'cuse me, do you mind if I sit here?"

I lift my head up, seeing the same woman from earlier, coffee now in hand and blond hair in her face. Her nervous anticipation melts into gentle recognition as our eyes meet.

"Oh, it's you." The words leave my mouth without much consideration.

"Yep, it's me." She gives me a small, awkward smile. "Can I sit?"

"Right, yeah. Sorry." I reach across the table and take my bag out of the chair. She sits, placing her coffee on the grated tabletop as I return my attention to my journal.

"*The Beast got all fucked up...*" No, that's way too negative. She's not gonna want to read that.

"*Devon and I hit a snag. We're stuck in Bumfuck, Colorado until we can get the Beast repaired. Oh, and I might be coming—*"

"What're you working on?" the woman asks over her cup.

"I'm trying to write a letter." I set the pen down in the center crease and slouch back in my chair. "But it's not really working."

"Sorry to hear that." She pulls her lips into a thin line as she takes a sip of coffee.

"Don't be," I mutter as I rip my straw free from its wrapper and stab it into my iced coffee. "It's not your fault."

She nods before taking another sip, gaze dropping into the cup.

Why must I always be stuck talking to strangers? Why can't I just act like a normal adult and pretend they don't exist? Instead, I just mumble small talk until one of us comes up with a good enough excuse to exit the conversation without coming off like an asshole.

"I like your journal. Very blue."

"It was a gift from the same person I'm writing to."

"How're you gonna send it if it's in a journal?"

That's a fair point, actually.

"I guess I'm not going to."

She sets her drink down then places both elbows on the table and rests her chin on her interlaced hands. "Why not?"

"She and I are in a bit of a rough patch right now. We aren't really speaking to each other."

Bit of an undersell there, I'd say.

"You aren't speaking, so you're writing to her. Yeah, that checks out. And if you're writing a letter, I'm guessing she's somewhere far away?"

"New York. The city."

The woman smiles, pleased with herself for guessing correctly. "So, you're here alone?"

"Well, yes and no." I sit up and lean forward, bringing my chest and hands to rest against the edge of the table. "I was with a friend, but... I guess he and I are in a pretty bad spot too."

She raises an eyebrow. "Sounds like a reoccurring motif."

Tell me about it.

"Yep. So that's why I'm here. Alone." I give her a shrug and a toothless smile before taking a pull from my own coffee. It tastes like dishwater and carbon with a touch of sugar. I lean back again, figuring this strange skeleton hunt in my closet has concluded.

"What happened with you and your friend?"

I give her a look that asks if she really wants to know. She smiles wide, showing off a pair of dimples to go with her perfect teeth.

"Come on, you can't leave me hangin' like that!"

Where to even begin?

I tell her about the road trip, hitting the pothole, busting the Beast's pump, and, of course, unloading on Devon.

"Sheesh," she exhales, leaning back in her chair. "That's some pretty hurtful shit, my dude."

"Yeah, I know. I was kinda lost in the sauce, and it just kept coming out. He caught me just right, and it was game over. But I've made my bed, so now I gotta lie in it, I guess. I doubt he'd be willing to hear me out, and he'd be right not to. I've been a real prick."

"What're you gonna do?"

"Finish my coffee, order an Uber, and fly home."

"To your girl, right? You'll fly in and sort everything out there at least, right?"

I crack a small, sardonic smirk. "Well..."

There really is no easy way to tell this story.

I tell her the whole situation, leaving out as many names as I can. I'm not really sure why—it's not like she's going to find these people—but it feels like the right thing to do. As I talk, she listens, occasionally blowing on or sipping at her drink. She laughs when I get to the bit with the Scent Killer but otherwise offers little until I finish.

"Sounds like you've made a real fuckin' mess, man." She laughs, and somehow, I can't help but join in. It isn't a mean laugh. It's the sort two coworkers might share while watching an entire shelf of books collapse after trying to put it together for two hours.

The laugh catches in my throat as I suddenly become acutely aware that I've just dumped copious amounts of deeply personal baggage on some random woman I met at a Starbucks maybe fifteen minutes ago.

"I'm sorry. I didn't mean to unload all this on you. I know it's a *lot.*"

"You're fine!" she assures me, fresh laughter bubbling out of her. "I'm the one who's prying. Besides, let's be realistic here: It's not like we're ever gonna run into each other again after this, so who cares?"

The perfect friend in my time of need turns out to be a stranger. Imagine that.

"So, what's your deal then? I've said my piece. Now you go."

Her eyes twinkle in the morning light as she leans forward to share. "There isn't much to tell. Small town girl drops out of college and comes back to home, totally lost. She struggles to find a job that fulfills her, or at least distracts her from the fact this is all there is until she either retires or dies."

"You must've been tons of fun at parties." I stick my tongue out at her. "What did you want to do? After college, I mean."

"No idea, but I wasn't about to waste sixty grand a year to figure it out. I'm just kinda playing it by ear now."

"Doesn't that scare you? Not knowing what's ahead?"

She laughs again, throwing her head back as if my question were the funniest joke she'd ever heard. "My dude, nobody knows what's ahead! Not me, not your friend, and certainly not you from how you've been batting."

I click my tongue and chuckle as she continues on.

"Seriously, you had a whole life planned out with this girl, and what's it gotten you?" She brings her fingers and thumb together to make a ring. "Fuck all. In fact, it sounds to me like it's costing you a lot more than just that relationship too."

"What'd you—" Out of the corner of my eye, I swear I see the Beast rolling down the street. My head snaps around, my heart in my throat. I expect to see Devon taking off out of Bumfuck, Colorado, leaving me to fend for myself, but it's just some other black car, barely half the size of the Beast. I let out the breath I hadn't realized I'd been holding.

"That." She points at me. " That's what I mean. You getting all worked up for a second there because you don't know how to reconcile your plans and what's actually happening."

I swallow my heart back down into my chest and turn my head back to her. "So, what am I supposed to do then?"

"Just let it come. Take the shit one day at a time. Never plan anything, *ever.*" She smiles, dimples pocking her soft, sharp cheeks again. "That one's a joke, but seriously. Just roll with it as it comes. Life's a lot more livable that way."

I don't know what to say, so we just sit in silence, sipping our drinks. For the first time since the start of this trip, my head feels clear. The ring of a cellphone breaks the silence as the woman takes her phone out and answers it.

"Mhmm, yeah, I'm still coming in. Had some issues come up, but I think they're sorted now." She looks at me and gives me a wink. I shoot back a thumbs up and immediately feel stupid, but she rolls her eyes and smirks. "Yeah, I can stay a little late to finish up. Okay. See you soon."

She hangs up and stands, pushing her chair in as she sidesteps it.

"Well, I'd better get to work, now that I'm running late. But I hope your mess gets sorted out... Jared, right?"

"Yeah, that's me."

"Well, *Jared*, if we ever cross paths again, I'll be expecting some bangin' advice. So, get to planning that."

"I definitely will...."

Oh my god. This woman swoops in, stops me from being the biggest shithead in the world, and I don't even remember her fuckin' name!

She must see the panic on my face as my pause stretches like cheap nylon.

"Relax, dude. Name's Amy, short for Amelia." She gives me a wave before turning to walk away, leaving me completely dumbstruck.

I couldn't have planned that if I tried.

I pull my phone out and type a message before I lose my nerve.

Can we talk? I push send and hope Devon won't kill me on sight.

Devon's waiting outside the repair shop as I walk up. He looks exhausted. My whole body feels numb as I approach possibly the most awkward conversation I will ever have.

"What's, uhh—how's the Beast doing?"

"Why? Having trouble booking an Uber?" he spits. "I thought you were catching a flight to be with Amelia, the most *important* person in your life."

Okay. He's pissed. Understandable.

"You could've just texted me about the car, so what do you want?"

A few mechanics mill around the parking lot, setting up cones and A-boards for something.

"Can we go for a walk? I wanna—"

"Oh! Now he wants to do something!" He forces a venomous laugh that sets my teeth on edge. "What do you wanna do, Jared? I'm just *dyin'* to know."

"Could we—"

"Nah, sorry. I don't feel well," he says in a nasal falsetto, clearly mocking me. "Let me ask Amelia first, see if it's okay for me to spend some time with my best friend." He turns and heads back toward the door.

"Devon, wait a second." I jog up and grab him by the shoulder. He spins on a dime, his face twisted into a visage of pure malice.

If looks could kill, I'd be a pillar of salt right now.

"Get your hand off me," he growls through gritted teeth.

I pull my hand back before he bites it off. "Devon, I just want to talk."

"I don't really give a fuck, *buddy*. If you wanna act like a piece of shit until you can get blackout drunk in New Orleans, you're more than welcome to, but you're out of your fucking mind if you think I'm gonna put up with it!"

A few of the staff are starting to notice our little scene as Devon continues to work himself up.

"I've been trying to do fun shit, but you just wanna act like a—"

"I blew it with Amelia." The words hit home. I can see it in the back of his hard, fiery eyes. "I blew the whole fuckin' thing, man, and I didn't know how to talk to you about it, and I'm sorry."

Devon's expression doesn't change; the harsh anger lines in his cheeks and forehead don't soften, but I can feel the atmosphere has shifted. He turns without a word and stomps back into the shop.

Should I go in after him? I know he's pissed as hell, but we need to talk. But I also don't wanna get punched in the head.

Before the door swings closed, Devon shoves it open again. "I'm starving. You're buying lunch." He shoves past me and continues on without looking back.

The walk down Main rings with deafening silence. Devon stares into each building as we pass, no doubt eager to let me stew until I make the first move.

"When you... After the party... I went to..."

Fuck me, this isn't gonna work.

"I've been keeping a lot of stuff to myself because I don't know how to tell you about it."

"I've noticed," he replies without looking my way. "Sometimes it's hard to tell the difference between when you're joking and when you're being a shit head. But you made it pretty obvious this time, shit head."

"I know!" I raise my voice, feeling a flash of anger shoot up from nowhere. I take a deep breath. Now isn't the time for more anger. "I know. The whole thing with Amelia was a wash, and—"

"A wash? What'd you mean, a wash?"

"Like I said, I blew it. I was way too fucked up and..." Flickers of Amelia standing there in front of me, silent and terrified, play out in my head. "And I ruined it. She and I haven't spoken since the night of the party."

"Hold up." Devon sticks his hand out in front of me, stopping me immediately. "I thought you said she didn't come to the party."

My face screws up as I speak the words I have been dreading this whole time. "I lied, Devon. I didn't come out to find you. I went because Amelia was going to go, with or without me, and I wasn't ready to lose out on my shot to tell her how I felt."

His expression shatters like a porcelain vase being hit with a sledgehammer as he staggers backward a few steps.

"I panicked in the moment because I didn't think I'd run into you, but of course, I did, and I didn't want to upset you even more than I already had." My stomach ties itself into knots as the words spill from me.

Devon says nothing and just stares at me with wide, dead eyes.

"I didn't know what else to do, so I lied, and I'm sorry! It was stupid and a waste because you were right, and I'm sorry I didn't see that, either."

Devon's gaze drops to the sidewalk as he crosses his arms, raising one hand to his lips to bite at his nails. He looks so fragile, as though if I breathe too hard, he might break apart.

Not this again. I can't handle this a second time.

"Devon, please say something," I beg. "Anything. Please."

"I don't even know what to say to you right now," he mutters, sandpaper voice rasping my already inflamed anxiety.

It's happening all over again.

"Wh-What can I do? What can I do to make it up to you?"

Devon's hand drops from his mouth as his head snaps up to lock eyes with me. "What can you do?" He walks right up to me, our noses about two inches apart. "How about you stop being so God damn *selfish*? How about you stop stepping on other people's toes to make your life easier, you *prick*! You're supposed to be my best friend; we're supposed to look out for each other! You have—"

The smallest inkling of a tear starts to well up in his eye as he takes a step back and brings the hem of his shirt up to wipe his face.

"You have no idea the kind of shit I've been going through for the last few months—hell, the last few *weeks*—because you've been too busy."

"Do you want to—"

"Stop."

The word instantly cinches my lips together.

"Jared, I can handle you being rude. I can even handle you being hostile. I shouldn't have to, but I can. You've seen me through some low points too. But this?" He lets out a little sickening chuckle, which makes my blood run cold. "This is beyond fucked up. Even for you." He puts a hand on my shoulder, fingers digging into my shirt and skin. "I'm sorry about what happened. I really am. But I need some time to process this... this fucking *insanity* you have just dropped on me."

For the second time today, I am left dumbstruck. I don't even know where to begin breaking down the mountain of words Devon just buried me under. His phone starts to ring, and he releases my shoulder. He puts it to his ear and takes a few steps away.

"Yes, you're speaking to him." The muffled voice on the other end of the line mumbles something in Devon's ear, but I can't make any of it out. "And that'll work for now? Perfect. We'll be right there." He hangs up and turns back to me. "Mechanic says they might have a quicker solution for us."

"That's great! I—" The excitement in my voice is undercut by guilt. "So, I'm back on the trip?"

"You were never off the trip, idiot." He starts to walk back up the road the way we came. "Luckily for you, I can't get this thing back to New York by myself, so I can't leave you here."

I jog up behind him but stop myself short of passing him. Devon leads the way back to Paul's in silence, hands held fast in his pockets, leaving me to wonder if he really would've left me behind.

TWELVE

After I stormed out on Devon, he spoke with the mechanics about expediting the repair on the pump. They told him if they could locate the leak and it was small enough, they might be able to patch it. It wouldn't be a permanent solution, but it would at least get us back to New York where we could have it properly fixed. Thankfully, they were able to do just that, and we were back on the road with only about three hours lost.

He also got in touch with Riley to explain what happened and that we'd be getting in super late. She completely understood and agreed to stay up and wait for us to arrive.

Now that the steering's working properly, I can focus on the talking Devon and I aren't doing. After explaining everything to me while he finished the paperwork and paid for the repair, he climbed in the back and hasn't said a word since. I flick my eyes from the road to the rearview mirror. He's still lounging in the loft, alternating between eating a sandwich and reading *House of Leaves*. It's been about five hours since we left Bumfuck. Only ten more to go. I pull my arm in from the window and take a drag on my smoke before sticking my whole arm back outside.

Consideration is key.

"Can we stop at the next gas station? I gotta piss." Devon's voice snakes out of the back seat and wraps around my neck like a noose.

"Sure," I choke out. "Could use some gas too."

I've been doing my best to keep up a brave face, but inside, my mind is flailing like a wolf caught in a trap.

First Amelia, now Devon. What if he gives up on me too? I've only got, like, two friends, and now they both think I'm the worst. They're not wrong, but shit, I'm trying to do better.

"Hey, can we talk about—"

"We already talked, didn't we?" His voice is flat and curt, face buried in his book.

"I know, but I'm worried you're gonna—"

"I'm gonna what?" He closes the book and holds it against his chest. "We've still got a good fifteen-hundred-ish miles to go until we get back to New York, and unlike you, I don't plan on leaving you to fend for yourself."

Our eyes meet in the rearview mirror. His are still sharp as ever, making me look away almost instantly.

"I wasn't really gonna leave you behind...." I say sheepishly.

"Doesn't much matter now," he says, opening *House of Leaves* back up. "So, why keep talking about it?"

I give a timid nod and go back to focusing on the road. *What a fucking nightmare I've made for myself.*

I never learned how to ride a bike as a kid. Fell over and got a boo-boo one too many times in the driveway, so I just said, "Fuck it. I'll just learn to drive."

My dad got me behind the steering wheel of his car twice before the divorce. I'd sit on his lap and steer while he handled the pedals. Both times were nearly disasters, but that didn't matter to me. I'd fallen in love with it.

As soon as I turned sixteen, I took my permit test and passed with flying colors. I could officially drive. As a reward, Dad let me drive us home from the DMV. I was excited and terrified all at once. I'd never driven on a real road before—I only ever practiced in parking lots—but Dad had confidence in me.

We ran through the checklist: wallet, seatbelt, mirrors, ignition. Check, check, check, and check. The steering wheel of his Jeep Wrangler vibrated in my hands, purring with anticipation. We did a couple laps in the parking lot, so I could get a feel for the drive before we hit the roads. Stop sign, turn signal, look left, look right. He squeezed my hand as I turned out.

We took the scenic route home. No highways, thankfully, and the most gorgeous trees Connecticut had to offer, or at least, so Dad said. He was blasting some country song, "Copperhead Road," I think, when he told me to pull over. Scared something had happened, I complied immediately. He looked me dead in the eye, and I'll never forget what he asked me.

"You wanna open this bad boy up?"

Several zippers, bolts, and screws later, and we're back on the road, doorless and roofless. I was worried the doors wouldn't fit in the trunk, but Dad just put the backseat down and stacked 'em up in there with the soft roof and windows.

I remember the wind. So loud and strong, whipping my hair all over the place. Seeing it dance in the side mirror made me laugh.

"This is freedom, son. The open road! The wind in your face! " He cranked the music back up, whooping and hollering along with the song.

We didn't get to see each other much. Dad only had custody on Wednesdays and every other weekend, but we made it count. Watching him rock along to the radio was the happiest I'd seen him in months. He was a free spirit, longing for something more than the banality his working life had to offer, and in these rare moments with me, I think he found it.

When we pulled into the driveway of his apartment building, he put one hand on my leg and told me he was proud of me. It wasn't the first time he'd said it to me, but it was the first time I believed it. Our time together driving was always the best. Just me, the open road, the wind on my face, and my proud father.

It's dark when I open my eyes. Proper dark. No-streetlights-or-moon-out dark. I roll onto my back and look straight up through the window at the night sky. It's clear and full of stars, not just the ten or twelve brightest you can see in New York or Los Angeles. Here, there had to be hundreds—thousands, maybe—of tiny pinpricks puncturing the dark sheet of night, only glimpsed between the passing silhouettes of trees and powerlines. It's beautifully eerie.

"Where are we?" I ask aloud, rubbing my eyes.

"About ten minutes out," Devon replies.

That can't be right. Devon took over after we gassed up the Beast right before we hit Kansas. It was still pretty light out, so that had to be around... four, maybe five? And I fell asleep maybe an hour or two after that. So...

I dig my phone out of my pocket and check the time. One-fifteen.

Holy shit. I slept for, like, five hours. I hope I can sleep later.

Riley moved back in with her parents after graduating so she could save money to get a place with Devon after he graduated. Devon always assured me there would be a place in their home for me to stay because I was just as important to him as she was. I always wondered if that bothered her. She never showed it if it did.

I wonder if that offer still stands, since I don't think I'll be living with Amelia anymore.

"Riley's parents are in Kansas City this week." Devon's eyes glint in the rearview mirror like the ruby eyes of the Shrike. "So it'll just be the three of us."

I grunt an acknowledgment and let out a big yawn. I sit up and stretch tall. My spine pops in three places, and it feels amazing.

Looking out the windshield, the headlights illuminate the fronts of pretty houses with little front lawns as we drive past. Quite a change from the squat houses of California and Arizona.

I guess it's easier to build tall houses when you don't have to worry about earthquakes. Do they get earthquakes in Arizona? No. So, why are the houses so short?

Devon parks the Beast in the driveway and hefts our suitcases out of the trunk. I'm on cooler duty, unfortunately. Devon's already inside the house by the time I get the first cooler out of the car. I lug it just in front of the garage and pop open the valve at the bottom, draining all the water out of it. I do the same with the second one, then drag them inside the garage for the night. I click the button to close the garage and head inside the house.

I'll be crashing in the basement since that's where Devon's set up my suitcase. The room's nice enough, and the futon's already been pulled out for me. Next to it is a door to a half-bathroom.

Nice, nice, nice.

I head out of the basement and up the stairs to the living room. Riley and Devon are sitting on the couch. Well, Riley is sitting on the couch, Devon is on his back with his head in her lap, filling her in about our trip so far.

I give her a small wave. "Hey, Riley."

"Good to see you, Jared." She scoops Devon's head off her lap so she can give me a hug. I tense up when she touches me. Amelia was the last person who hugged me. That feels so far away now, like a lifetime ago, but somewhere deep inside me, I still feel a touch of guilt for letting someone else hug me.

"Devon was telling me about the Scent Killer you picked up in Phoenix. Absolutely too funny! I would've done the exact same thing."

Devon waves an arm at her, playfully demanding attention. She sits back down, returning his head to its rightful spot.

"Tell Jared the plan," he coos, rolling over so his face is against her stomach.

"Right! So, we're going to Hannibal tomorrow, where Mark Twain grew up. I'm pretty sure you already knew about that."

I nod. Devon had *insisted* we go visit. I'm not a huge Mark Twain fan like him, but history is always cool, so I agreed to go along. Plus, they have a bunch of antique shops, and I do love a good antique.

"Then the next day, we're gonna hit St. Louis. I know you've never been, Jared, so we can hit the Gateway Arch and all those other fun, touristy spots. Plus, there are some really nice parks we can rent bikes to ride through. Devon mentioned you might like that."

The thought of biking anywhere makes my heart hurt. *Just another Amelia thing I have to struggle through with a strong face.*

"And we can play that morning by ear. If we're out late drinking, we can just take a lazy morning, or we can do something local if we're still in one piece." She laughs at her own joke.

I manage a weak smile with Amelia on my mind. "That all sounds wonderful, Riley."

"I think so! Even if *somebody* won't give me any input!" She runs her hands through Devon's hair, shaking his head back and forth.

"Stoooooop," he moans into her midsection. Riley giggles while I look on with tired eyes.

"We're gonna stay up for a bit, have a couple beers. You're welcome to join in if you'd like."

"Thanks, Riley, but I'm just really beat. Long day, long drive. You know."

"Oh, sure, sure," she replies, nodding. "You saw the spread for you downstairs?"

"Yeah, I scoped it out."

"Perfect! We'll see you in the morning."

We exchange goodnights, and I head down. I fetch my toiletries kit, brush my teeth, and change into some comfy pajama pants. The futon is surprisingly comfortable, but the mattress has a weird slope, forcing me to lie diagonally across it. I plug my phone in and slip under the covers.

With Amelia rattling around in my brain, a bad idea takes shape as I close my eyes. I try to push it away but trying to ignore it just makes it stick even more.

Fuck it.

I roll over and grab my phone. I haven't rubbed one out in, like, a week. Amelia's page is still open from the last time I prowled Facebook. I know she posted some beach photos last summer that'll be perfect for a bit of self-pitying masturbation. I swipe down to refresh the page while I untie my drawstring. As it loads in, the first thing I notice is her new profile picture. It's her and Rory, sitting in the grass at Bryant Park. She's sitting in between his outstretched legs, leaning into his chest. His arms are wrapped around her, and his head rests on hers.

I scroll down and see it: *Amelia Taylor is in a relationship with Rory Kleine.* Posted yesterday. My heart implodes, and I wish the rest of me would too.

THIRTEEN

Hannibal, Missouri, is a picturesque slice of days gone by, nestled right on the bank of the Mississippi River. Mark Twain spent a good part of his young life growing up here, and it shows. Hannibal inspired the setting of his most famous works, *The Adventures of Tom Sawyer* and *The Adventures of Huckleberry Finn*.

I'm more partial toward Pudd'nhead Wilson, *but there I go, being all closed-minded again.*

Devon and Riley change poses as I take another picture of them in front of the Tom Sawyer and Huck Finn statue. I look at the photo, noticing the waffle cone they've been sharing has dripped on Devon's shirt between shots. I choose to keep it to myself, hopeful they won't make me retake any of the pictures. Watching them fawn over each other makes my soul hurt. I haven't told either of them about last night. Don't want to spoil the fun.

Riley beams as she takes back her phone.

"How do they look?" Devon asks, sucking a mouthful of melting ice cream from the cone.

"We're looking hot as hell," she says with a smirk. "Do you want me to take any of you two?"

I squirm and shake my head.

"We can if you want," Devon says, holding his hand over his eyes to block out the sun. "I don't care either way."

"I'm okay. I'm not really in the picture-taking mood anyway," I tell Riley, which actually translates to, "I'd rather forget this day ever happened because I feel like my skin's been stretched too tightly over a black hole in the process of consuming everything I hold dear."

She doesn't seem to pick up on the translation.

I shift my gaze from her to the ground. I can't bring myself to look at Devon right now. Every time I do, I'm reminded of what an asshole I am, and that manages to make me feel just a little bit worse, which is pretty remarkable at this point.

He's been acting much nicer to me since we got to Riley's, but I'm not sure if that's for her sake or mine.

"That's fine! We don't have to take any more here," Riley chirps. "Where to next?"

"We could go see the Tom Sawyer fence," Devon replies. He passes the dripping waffle cone to Riley, who reluctantly accepts it. He shakes the ice cream off his hand before producing a small fold-up map of the town from his pocket. We'd picked it up in one of the little antique shops along the way. "I'm pretty sure it's close by."

As Riley and Devon pour over the map, my attention drifts from the unfeeling, metallic eyes of Tom and Huck to the street ahead of us.

North Main Street is a juxtaposition of old hand-laid brick and mortar buildings with Honda Accords, wrought-iron street signs, and solar-powered parking meters. The old and new clash with violent beauty. I pull out and light a smoke.

Amelia would've loved this. At least, I think she would, but it's hard to know what's true with her now. How many other parts of our relationship were just fabrication? How much was real interest and romance, and how much was just toleration for the sake of staving off solitude? This woman, who meant so much to me, now feels like nothing more than a stranger. How am I supposed to feel? What am I supposed to do?

"What'd you think, Jared?" Devon's voice turns my head toward them. I wipe the other thoughts away.

"Sorry, I was spacing out. What're we doing?"

"Riley wants to hit up Rockcliffe Mansion, but I wanna go see the fence."

"So, like, is it just a fence? Or... what?"

"No, there's more," Devon asserts, holding up the map for me to see. "There's a whole museum attached to Twain's old house too. They've got all sorts of cool stuff about his books and life in there."

"That does sound pretty cool."

"See?" He turns to Riley, giving her the gotcha face. "That's what I said!"

She rolls her eyes and giggles. "Lead on then, gentlemen!" she booms as we walk out of Tom and Huck's small park and up onto North Main.

The Mark Twain Boyhood Home and Museum was only about four blocks down from the statue. As we walk up, Riley makes the executive decision to pitch the rest of Devon's ice cream soup before he makes a complete mess of himself. I purchase three tickets, then rejoin the group to distribute them. They're standing in a short line, waiting to get their picture taken in front of the fence.

"If you guys wanna head inside, I can catch up with you," Devon tells us as I hand out the tickets. "I need to get at least my picture taken with it."

"What is your deal with this fence?" A little chuckle bubbles up from me as I ask.

"It's literally the fence from Tom Sawyer. This is *the* fence Tom tricked all the other kids into whitewashing for him." Devon beams as he talks. "I've read that scene so many times, and now I'm actually here, in front of it!" The last time I saw Devon this happy was at the observatory, before... yeah. It's nice to see my friend smile again.

"I didn't know you liked *Tom Sawyer* this much."

"It's one of my favorite books. Read it all the time growing up. My dad used to read *Tom Sawyer* to me when I was a baby. Told me I'd always get all giggly during the fence painting bit. I promised him I'd get a picture with it for him." He gets a little misty-eyed while I struggle to picture Devon being giggly at any age.

"Are you sure you don't mind?" Riley asks him.

"Yeah. If you guys wanna head inside, don't let me stop ya."

"A little A/C might be nice," she offers to me with a shrug.

"Yeah, I could get behind that."

The two of us head inside, leaving Devon in line to enjoy his fence.

Once inside, Riley and I split up to explore the museum at our own pace. I make my way over to the recreation steamboat deck along the far wall. According to the plaques, Twain worked as a steamboat captain for a bit, and apparently, he really enjoyed it.

I might not be the biggest fan of Mark Twain, but I've got to admit, the guy lived a pretty cool life. Plus, enjoying a job? Truth really is stranger than fiction.

The museum is surprisingly empty for Hannibal's main attraction, but I'm perfectly happy to have the steamboat deck all to myself. I make my way around to the ship's helm and, more importantly, to the ship's wheel. Grasping the spokes in my hands, I can almost hear the ocean waves.

Well, the Mississippi waves, anyway. Still plenty of freedom and adventure on the Mississippi.

Amelia knew how much I loved the ocean. I made it pretty clear on our first trip to Jones Beach the summer we first met. The ship's wheel hurts to hold, sharp with bitter regret. All I can think of is the little charm on my journal and all the stories the two of us will never share. They flash through my mind like lightning in a storm, but I hold fast to the wheel. I can steer through this storm.

I was still angry with my mom for the divorce when she remarried, so it's not too hard to believe I had a lot of issues with my new stepdad. Mom knew I liked the ocean, liked the distant, strange allure that comes with something so vast and unknowable, so she always pushed for him and me to go out on his fishing boat. I think she figured it would help me warm up to him.

Finally, I relented when she threatened to take away my PlayStation 2 if I didn't go out at least once. He and I made the long drive to the port in Niantic, loaded up with rods, reels, and tackle. We got the boat set up and made our way out onto the Long Island Sound.

I was determined to not only have no fun but also to speak as little as humanly possible. Couldn't have this strange man think I was enjoying our time together. I sat on a little seat near the back of the boat, pouting like the petulant child twelve-year-old Jared was, and watched him drive the boat. Instead of a regular steering wheel, he installed a small ship's wheel to use. I always thought it was cool, even if I didn't say so.

Once we got out into the open waters, he asked me if I wanted to drop a line. I told him I wanted to go home, so he made me a deal: We could turn around and go home if I drove. In hindsight, that was stupidly clever of him, much too clever for my tiny, preteen brain. So I agreed and took the wheel.

Driving a boat is much different than driving a car. Of course, I didn't know that at the time, but looking back, it's obvious. If driving on the open road is freedom, driving on the ocean is understanding the infinite number of opportunities that freedom permits. After showing me how the throttle worked, my stepdad set me free to pilot us home.

Much to my chagrin, it was amazing. It only took five minutes of ripping donuts and catching air off tall waves for my anger to slip from my mind. Feeling the salty air draw both moisture and frustration from me, I couldn't help but start to laugh.

We went out every weekend of that summer. He and I still had a long way to go, but we had finally found some common ground in that rustic ship's wheel.

I crank the steamboat's wheel far to the left, piloting around imagined obstacles in the river.

I think I'd like to own my own boat one day. A big one, like this, but with a gas engine. I can't even begin to figure out how steam power works. I could take all my friends out. Devon and Riley would be game... Well, at least Riley would be. Devon might just tag along. I think Kat likes the beach, and what is a boat but a sand-free, 360-degree beach? Maybe even Jess would tag along after giving me an ass whooping for ditching her. I miss my friends. All of my friends.

I try to think of the last time I spent time with friends who weren't Amelia. The last time I went to the beach, or the Cheesecake Factory, or just bummed around the house with someone else, but I can't. I look around the empty boat deck.

Spent all that time with Amelia, and look what it got me.

"Permission to come aboard, Captain?"

I turn my attention to the middle gangway, one of three planks that connect the elevated boat deck to the museum floor, where Devon stands.

"Permission granted."

He saunters aboard as I return my gaze over the bow with measured speed. I don't want him to think I'm avoiding him while avoiding him.

"If you want a turn at the wheel, I can—"

"You're fine," he says, waving a hand at me.

He makes his way around the deck, glancing at a couple of the info plaques and examining the woodwork. I follow him with my eyes. He's got his hands pushed deep into his pockets. His shoulders are tense, practically pushed up to his ears. He looks nervous about something.

Nothing good, I'm sure.

Devon turns around quickly and catches me staring at him. I dart my eyes away as fast as I can, but he's definitely noticed. He steps toward me, and I brace for impact.

"Jared, I can tell you're buggin' out, so I'll be quick. Okay?"

I nod sheepishly, feeling tiny and anxious.

"I'm not ready to forgive you. You've said and done an incredible amount of shitty things over the last few days—well, last few weeks—and I'm still processing that."

He pauses to nibble at his thumbnail.

"But I'm not angry at you."

Plot twist.

"I talked it over with Riley, and, being my better half, she made some good points in your favor." He leans against one of the beams supporting the canopy over the helm.

Part of me wants to know what that silver-tongued woman could've possibly said to persuade him. But another part is just fine with leaving it alone and enjoying the moment.

"So, where does that leave us?" My mouth is dry from a mixture of worry and hope.

"I'm not really sure yet, but I'm hoping we'll wind up somewhere better than where we've been lately." He takes one hand out of his pocket and extends it to me.

"So, we're going with extra-cheesy," I say, making us both crack a smile.

"Just shake the damn hand," he says, chuckling.

I do, and for the first time all day, Amelia fades from my conscious thoughts.

We get back in line to take some extra goofy group photos in front of Devon's fence, then walk around to find some antique shops to hit up for nifty shit. By the time we pile back into the Beast, I've purchased an ancient pewter teapot with matching cream and sugar dishes. Devon bought a couple of turquoise glass telegraph insulators. Being the brains of our merry band, Riley made the smart choice and didn't buy junk to clutter her room because she is *lame*. Even Devon agreed.

We get on the road and make our way back to Riley's place for a much-needed night of drinking and lechery. Riley reclines in the loft while Devon and I sing along to "Africa" by Toto. We belt the high notes shamelessly since we can barely be heard over the rush of wind through the open windows

"Why can't you guys listen to normal music?" Riley shouts up to us.

"Can't you just enjoy it like a normal person?" Devon asks, looking at her in the rearview.

"No!" she bellows, dropping her voice into her chest for added gravitas. We laugh so hard, I start coughing.

Devon parks the Beast in the driveway, and we all head inside for some heavy drinking, laughing, and general dipshittery.

By the time I stagger downstairs to bed, absolutely piss drunk, I can't help but giggle with excitement for our adventures in St. Louis. I faceplant into the futon and immediately pass out from both exhaustion and intoxication.

My phone vibrates against my face, making my head throb angrily. Drunk Jared decided not to have any water before passing out, so now I get to pay for that. I crack open one eye to see who on earth could be calling me.

It's a New York number, but it's not saved in my phone. Who the hell... Oh, fuck!

I bolt upright and clear my throat before answering. "Hello?"

"Hi! Is this Jared?"

"This is he."

"Hi, Jared, this is Patricia, from Chase Bank. How're you today?"

I'm hungover as fuck, Patricia, and your voice is grating. How're you?

"Doing fine." I press the heel of my hand into my temple and work it in a circle.

"That's great." Patricia types away at a keyboard. Each stroke rings out like the firing of an automatic rifle. I pull the phone a few inches away from my ear. "So, the person we hired you to replace has to leave earlier than expected. I wanted to ask if you could start a little earlier."

Oh, great. I haven't even started yet, and they're already trying to consume my life.

"Uhh... When did you have in mind?"

"Would you be able to start this coming Wednesday, the thirty-first?"

That's our last day in New Orleans, and I'll be fucked if I'm cutting even a second of our week in that blessed place.

"I can't do that day, but I could do the... third? Fourth? That Saturday."

"Yes, the third." Patricia taps away at her keyboard, making me pull the phone away again. "That would be fine. So I'll get that in for you, and we'll see you on the third at eight o'clock in the morning."

Fuck me. Nothing like doing math at 8:00 a.m. to hammer home how miserable this is gonna be.

"See you then. Buh-bye."

I hang up the phone and drop it on the futon next to me. So, now I start on the third instead of the seventh. I guess New Orleans really will be my last hurrah before selling my soul off to our corporate deities.

Three days to haul ass from New Orleans to New York is gonna be tight. We'll be fine. Bourbon Street alone will be well worth the haul for Devon and me both.

I take in a shaky breath and stalk into the bathroom. My body feels like a desiccated corn husk. My mouth: bone dry. My eyes: beet red. My skin: sandpaper. I flick on the faucet and drink deep from the tap.

God, I've missed well water. No funky, chlorine, recycled pool water taste out here in Missouri.

After a few big, much-needed gulps of cold water, I wipe my mouth on the back of my hand and head upstairs to find the others.

Climbing the stairs is far more daunting than anticipated. I crawl up into the living room, parched and breathing heavily. I shuffle into the kitchen, fetch a glass from the drying rack, and fill it. Four more glasses of water later, I feel like I might not turn to dust. I set the glass back in the rack.

It's way too quiet in here. Where'd Devon and Riley go? They should be up by now.

I strain my ears, trying to hear them over the sound of my own heartbeat thrumming in my head. Nothing. I notice a pan half full of eggs, half full of bacon sitting on a cold burner.

Did they forget something for breakfast and run out?

I shuffle over to the couch, but just as I sit, I hear a muffled voice. I can't tell if it's Devon or Riley, though. With a groan, I stand up from the couch and make my way past the stairs into the hall. Riley's room is situated at the end, past the upstairs bathroom and her parents' room. As I approach, I swear I can hear hushed voices through the cracked door. No, just one voice, but I can't tell if it's Devon or Riley talking. I tap a knuckle gently on the door before pushing it open.

Devon's sitting on the edge of the bed, phone pressed to his ear, while Riley sits next to him and rubs his back with one hand. She looks at me with dark eyes.

"What's going on?" I mouth to her.

Before she can answer, Devon speaks to whoever's on the other end of his call. "I'll borrow Riley's laptop and look at flights right now, or I can look on my phone. It really doesn't matter." His voice is all bent out of shape. He takes a quick, uneasy breath. "I gotta go. I'll text you updates."

He ends the call and brings the phone down into his lap, staring at the screen. It slips between his fingers and lands on the carpeted floor between his legs. I watch with curious concern as he cups his face in his hands then slowly drags them down as if he were trying to peel off his own face.

"What's going on? What're you looking up flights for?"

Devon looks up at me with puffy, red eyes. "My dad's in the hospital."

Devon's words hit me like a brick in a pillowcase. "Wait, wha—how did this happen?"

Devon drops his gaze back to the floor and takes in a long, quivering breath. "We knew this could happen, but we didn't expect it to." His voice is barely a whisper.

"Whoa, whoa, whoa." I cross the room and sit on the other side of Devon. "What'd you mean, you knew this might happen?"

Riley's face betrays her surprise as she shoots him a look. "You didn't tell him, did you?"

Devon shakes his head.

"Okay, guys, seriously. What the fuck is going on?" Worry mutates into fear as I flick my eyes back and forth between the two of them. Devon won't even look at me.

"His dad's sick, Jared. Really sick. It'd been pretty manageable for a while, but recently, about three weeks ago, it got worse."

"Jesus Christ..."

Wait a second, three weeks ago? That would've been while I was working on Amelia's... Oh, fuck me.

"They put him on a more aggressive treatment, but it's really hard on his whole system. Lots of possible side effects: weakened immune system, brittle bones, even—"

She looks at Devon and stops. Fresh tears glisten on his cheeks as he clenches his jaw so tightly, his head shakes.

"Broken hip trumps weakened immune system. Mom said he's about to go into surgery." He wipes his face on his sleeve before sniffling loudly.

Riley grimaces and gets up. "I'm gonna get you some tissues, okay?"

"Okay." Devon's voice is completely dead. None of the warmth or excitement it usually carries. Now it's just air passing through tubes to make sound. Just empty enunciation.

As Riley leaves the room, I can't help but press him. "Why didn't you tell me about this?"

"When would I have, Jared?" His voice cuts right through me. It's low and sad and oh-so-fragile. "You were preoccupied with Amelia's shit. I just hoped we could've done what we always did. Go out to a party, or a movie, or play some games, or something normal. Something to distract me."

Riley comes back and hands the box of tissues to Devon. "Do you want me to finish making breakfast, or do you want me to wait for you?" she asks, cupping his cheek in one hand.

"If you're hungry, you should eat. My appetite's gone."

Never thought I'd hear that.

He takes a tissue and loudly blows his nose.

Riley gives him a small smile and kisses his cheek. "Love you," she says as she steps back out of the room. "Grab me if you need anything."

"Love you too," Devon replies softly. He balls up the used tissue and hucks it into the trash bin across the room. "Swish," he chuckles, flashing me a sad smirk I wish I could return.

"I'm sorry, Devon," I tell him gravely.

His smile fades as his eyes drift back to the floor. "Y'know, I was fine with you bailing on me to see her at first. I remember how much time Riley and I spent together during the first few months of our relationship, so I figured it was just natural. But somewhere along the way, it felt like..." Devon moves his hands as if he were sifting through a pile of clothing for one particular sock, "like something shifted. Like it wasn't just about spending time with her but spending time away from me. You didn't wanna do anything anymore. You just bummed around the house, waiting for Amelia to whisk you away."

He leans forward, planting his elbows on his knees and rubbing his forehead. At this point, I'm not sure if he's still talking to me or just talking.

"What was I supposed to do? How could I have told you and not push you even further away?" He covers his face with his hands. "I kept thinking, 'We just need to get on the trip. It'll all work out once we get on the road,' but now...." His voice breaks as the sentence trails off.

Regret settles in my stomach like a cold stone.

This whole time I was isolating myself from him. And all the family phone calls, wanting to go out, and pestering me over and over and over again to do something. God, I let him down so bad.

"What do we do now?" I keep my voice as even as I can.

"I don't know." Devon lifts his head and grabs another tissue. "Mom wants me to fly back as soon as I can, but I have no idea how long I'll be gone." He looks at me with the guiltiest eyes I've ever seen. I can tell he needs to say something but doesn't know how. They're the same eyes I had in Bumfuck.

"Devon, just say what's on your mind, man."

He gives a weak nod. "D'you think we could shift the New Orleans stop back a few days?" He sucks in a quick breath, eager to qualify the problematic question. "I know it'll be a pain, but I'm sure you could stay here for the time being, and I know you don't start work until the seventh, so there'd be time. Right?"

"I had to move my start date to the third," I say, dropping my gaze to the floor. I can't look at him as I rob yet more hope from his already plundered vaults. "They called me this morning. I was coming up to tell you guys."

Devon wilts like a dying flower, sagging into the mattress. The silence hangs heavy, neither one of us sure what to say next. Suddenly, he jumps up, grabs the tissue box, and whips it at the wall across the room. It hits with a surprisingly loud whack, making me flinch.

"What a fucking waste!" he yells before crumbling to the floor. I get down on my knees and shift up next to him, resting a hand on his back. He's breathing long, stuttering breaths, his whole body shaking as he quietly tries to hold it together.

Riley throws open the door but stops short of racing in when she sees us. I point to the now caved-in tissue box, to which she nods.

"What if I could get the Beast back to New York by myself? That wouldn't be a waste, would it?" I look over to Riley. "How long a drive is it from here to New York?"

She takes out her phone and taps away. "It's about fifteen hours, give or take, with traffic."

That is gonna be one shitty drive.

"But what about New Orleans?" Devon mumbles. "What about the hotel, and the museums, and—"

"You worry about getting home. I'll take care of New Orleans. Okay?"

Even I'm surprised with how confident that sounded.

I snake my arm under his shoulder and slowly stand him back up. "It's gonna be okay, all right? Go with Riley and get your flight stuff sorted, and I'll get the rest figured out. Okay?"

Devon slowly nods and mouths "okay" as Riley takes his hand and leads him out of the room, closing the door behind them. A strange peace pervades the air as I fall back onto Riley's bed, a sort-of calm before the storm.

Is there any other way we can swing this? It's too late to change the hotel, and most of those museum tickets are non-refundable. Plus, there's no way of knowing when Devon'll be back, and I would really rather not still be here by myself whenever Riley's parents come home.

I stare up at the ceiling fan, counting the little black dots on each blade, just like I did with Jess's.

Get the car, see New Orleans. That was how we planned it all those months ago. Every other stop was just another stepping stone to get us closer to Louisiana, but now, here we are. Maybe Devon was right. This was a huge waste...

I squeeze my eyes shut and breathe, riding each one like a wave. Up and down, up and down. Always up and down with me, stuck in a never-ending spiral. Just like those little black dots. Always being moved without ever moving themselves, at the mercy of the fan blade.

I'm so tired of ups and downs. I need to move in a different direction. Forward might be nice for a change.

I sit up and open my eyes. I start making a list in my head of things to do: cancel the hotel, cancel the tickets for the Cabildo and New Orleans Pharmacy Museum, and cancel the dinner reservations for each night.

I open up my phone and start looking up phone numbers.

There'll always be another chance to see New Orleans, even if work eats up most of my time. I just have to take it as it comes, like Amel—Amy said.

FOURTEEN

After several phone calls and even more polite apologies, I emerge from Riley's room. Both of them are sitting at the island with her laptop in front of them.

"Everything's canceled," I announce. "Even got a full refund from the hotel."

"How'd you manage that?" Riley lifts her gaze from the screen to look at me.

"Called them first and moved our stay three weeks out. Then hung up and called all the other places. Then called the hotel again, got a different person, and canceled it without an issue since it was three weeks out."

"That actually worked?" Her brows furrow in surprise.

Of course, it didn't actually work. They charged me half the price in fees, but I don't want Devon feeling any worse than he already does.

"Course it did, because I am brilliant." I flash all eight hundred of my teeth in a huge, dumb grin. "Any luck finding a flight?"

"We found one that leaves at seven o'clock tonight. It's a non-stop flight too."

I look over at the clock on the stovetop. It's 11:23 a.m. right now, so we've still got a while to kill.

"All right. So, we should leave around four to get there with enough time for Devon to get through security, then I can drop you back off and hit the road."

She nods, and I head toward the stairs so I can start repacking.

"There's another flight," Devon says suddenly, stopping me in my tracks. He's gotten his voice back. "It leaves at eight o'clock tomorrow morning."

"Babe, don't start with this again," Riley asserts. "Just buy the seven o'clock one before it fills up."

"Why would you want a later flight?" I ask, stepping back into the kitchen.

"Because it leaves from New York." He turns to look at me, so I can tell he's serious.

"Devon—"

"No, Riley!" he interrupts harshly. Devon must sense the sudden awkwardness as Riley and I look at each other. "Sorry. Jared and I planned this trip, paid for this trip, and started this trip. We are damn well going to finish it." He turns back to the screen. "Dad's a tough bastard. If he's gonna die, he can at least wait a few extra hours for me."

"Devon!" Riley blurts. "Don't be so morbid."

I cross the room to stand behind him. He's pulled up the flight page and started plugging his info in. "Are you sure about this, dude?"

"I told you in Colorado, Jared, I have no intention of leaving you behind." He looks me dead in the eye, and I can tell he means it.

"Okay. We need to get going then. We need to be on the road as soon as possible. Riley, can you...?"

I look at Riley across the island. With her hands on her hips, she looks like an angry mother preparing to scold her children for being too stubborn, but her soft eyes reveal the worry.

"Can you help me load the coolers into the Beast?"

"You two are impossible." She sighs, shaking her head.

"That's why we're best friends." I look at Devon and catch the slightest twinkle of that familiar boisterousness in his dark eyes. "Right?"

"You're god damn right," he affirms, patting at his pajamas for a moment before hopping up and heading back toward Riley's room.

"Well, let's get you all set," Riley says, dropping her hands and coming around the island.

"Babe! Where's my wallet?" Devon calls from the room.

She and I look at each other before turning to look at Devon's wallet, sitting on the island next to the laptop. We share a knowing smile as we head into the garage.

We load the empty coolers into the back and toss the blanket and pillows back over them. Riley follows me into the basement to repack my suitcase. I throw dirty and clean clothes together and fold the case closed. I have to sit on it to get it to zip, but it works. Riley hands me my toiletries case, which I toss in my satchel for fear of being unable to get the suitcase closed again. I wheel the red case out and toss it in the trunk.

"Devon, how's it coming?" I yell up the stairs as I come back in.

"I'm coming, I'm coming," he calls, lumbering down his own case. "I had to wait for the confirmation email to go through."

"Go start the car. I gotta piss." I slip past him and into the basement bathroom. I can hear the Beast roar to life as I flush the toilet. I grab my satchel bag off the pull-out and head outside.

I hop in the driver's seat and adjust my mirrors. Devon and Riley are talking about something, but I can't hear them over the noisy exhaust. Devon hefts his suitcase up and tosses it in, shaking the whole car.

"Easy back there, killer!" Our eyes meet in the rearview, and I smile at him. He rolls his eyes and slams the trunk.

We've still got a little over half a tank, which should be enough to get us well into Illinois. Devon opens the passenger door, and I toss the satchel into the loft.

"Ready?" I ask him.

"As I'll ever be."

Before I can throw the Beast in reverse, Riley knocks on my window.

"What's up?" I ask as I roll it down.

"I told Devon to text me when you guys get to JFK, but I know his head's like a sieve, so make sure you remind him."

"You hear what she's saying about you?" I ask my copilot.

"I do, but I'm a little caught up trying to remember who she is."

She flips him off, and we all laugh. For a moment, all the bad shit going on seems to disappear.

"Drive safe, you two." Riley pats the window frame twice before heading back toward the house.

I shift into reverse and roll out of the driveway onto the street.

Here we go.

Halfway through the second hour, I'm feeling the hangover start to creep in again. The sun is just a bit too bright, even with sunglasses, the GPS is just a touch too shrill, and a dull ache pulses at the back of my head like Morse code.

You feel like shit, stop. You should stop drinking, stop. Maybe you should've eaten some breakfast, full stop.

"I'm gonna stop at the next station. I think I need something to eat, and we definitely need gas." I look over at Devon, who's looking a little green himself. "You look like shit."

"Well, I feel pretty shitty. Some snackage sounds perfect."

"Look on the GPS and see if there's anywhere nearby."

The distance between gas stations on the I-70 is obnoxious beyond words. It would be faster to pit stop at the bottom of the ocean and dig our own crude oil to refine. After another thirty-five minutes of uncomfortable driving, we finally arrive at a 7-Eleven. We park at a pump and shamble out of the Beast. Devon roams the salty-snacks aisle while I make my way to the singular drink cooler in the back.

What kind of self-respecting 7-Eleven only has one drink cooler? What kinda operation they running here?

I scan the shelves, looking for something to squelch this icky grossness quickly overtaking me.

Water? Nah. Coke? No. Sprite, Dr. Pepper, Fanta, orange juice... Nothing.

Just before giving up, my eyes settle on a bottle of milk on the bottom row.

Milk's good for you, right? It's got carbs, fats, protein, the whole works. When was the last time I had just milk, no cereal or chocolate syrup or anything? I dunno.

I pull out the pint of milk and take it up to the counter. Devon walks up next to me and slaps a bag of Chex Mix down next to my milk. We pay and head outside.

"Did you seriously buy *only* milk?" He shoots me a weird look and chuckles.

"Hell yeah, I bought milk. It's got everything a body needs. Haven't you seen the commercials?" I crack the seal on the plastic bottle and pull the top off. "Plus, it'll make my bones happy, and happy bones make a happy Jared." I take a long sip of the moo juice as Devon stares at me.

"That's ominous as shit, dude." He rips open the bag of Chex Mix with his teeth, spitting the ripped bit in the trash bin.

As the liquid trickles down my throat, I feel the macronutrients begin their relief campaign throughout my body. My headache, gone; the light sensitivity, gone; my exhaustion, completely *fucking* gone. Shit, I might even be getting a little hard. My third-eye chakra has opened, and I have achieved nirvana outside a 7-Eleven in Illinois.

"Holy shit," I mumble to myself. Looking at how much I have left, I realize I just drank half the bottle in one go.

"Is it spoiled?"

I shake my head and extend the bottle toward him.

"Jared, I'm not falling for it."

"It's not expired, wank-stain. Just drink it."

Devon takes the bottle and hesitantly raises it to his lips. He shoots me an if-this-is-actually-spoiled-you're-gonna-be-wearing-it look and takes a small sip. His eyes slowly grow wider as he drinks more and more. A deep, soulful sigh leaps from his lips as he finishes the bottle.

"Holy shit."

"That's what I'm saying!"

Devon turns around and heads back toward the station. "You pump the gas. I'm getting my own!" he hollers to me.

I refill the Beast, and we get back on the road, bellies full of milk and Chex Mix. Truly, a breakfast fit for kings.

Hour six of fifteen. Our milk-fueled ecstasy burnt out about an hour ago while we were in traffic outside of Indianapolis. Devon fell asleep in the passenger seat a little while ago, and I am struggling to stay awake in the late afternoon heat. I pull off into an empty scenic view lot on the side of the highway.

Devon wakes up as I turn the Beast off. He yawns and stretches as I hop out and do some standing stretches of my own. My ass is completely numb, and my legs feel like they're about to fall off.

I walk around a bit, feeling sensation return to my lower cheeks as fresh blood circulates around my uncrumpled bottom half. I look out past the guard rail into an enormous field full of young corn stalks, probably about up to my neck.

So much for scenic. I've always wanted to run around in a cornfield, but I'm terrified of getting lost. Plus, who knows what could be hiding in there past the first few rows. I guess this one isn't too bad, since I can see over it still. But in a few months, forget it. Ain't no aliens gonna get me in there.

The stalks sway in the summer breeze as the eager buzz of insects waiting for twilight surrounds me. Getting caught out here after dark would surely mean a swift death by exsanguination from all the mosquitos. I swat at my neck as I feel one land. The sun has begun its descent for the day. Although the telltale burnt oranges and saturated purples of early evening aren't out yet, the vibrant yellow afternoon light has begun to mellow into a less blinding orange.

"Hey, Jared?" Devon calls in a trembling voice. Fearing something's happened, I spin around and see he's out of the cab, leaning against the Beast's front bumper. He's staring at his phone with this thin-lipped look of worry. "Did you see this?"

He turns the phone, revealing Amelia's Facebook page. My stomach twists a bit, but I tough it out.

"Yeah. Saw it the night before Hannibal. Our first night at Riley's." As I tell him this, the worry on his face melts into concerned surprise.

"Why didn't you say anything?"

Because I was scared of upsetting you? Scared of ruining the fun of being in Hannibal?

"If I kept it to myself, I could pretend it wasn't real. Just my tired brain inventing some hurtful daydream. Saying it out loud would've meant I had to face it." I sit on the guard rail in front of the Beast and kick at some small stones on the asphalt. "But I can't keep running from it, can I? Besides, I know you don't really like her, so..." My voice trails off as I shrug.

"It's not that I don't like her," Devon starts carefully. "I don't—well, *didn't*—like the way she made you treat other people. Every minute of your day had to be open, just in case she wanted to see you. But if you wanted to see her? 'Sorry, I've already got plans.' Y'know?"

I nod slowly.

I've wasted enough of my life waiting around for her. Sometimes I forget how observant Devon can be. It's almost like we're best friends.

"Do you mind taking over for a while? I think I'd like to close my eyes for a bit."

"Sure, sure." He tucks his phone away and pulls open the driver's door while I take one last look at the big, open sky. "I'm sorry this went so sideways, Jared. All of this."

I exhale a tiny laugh through my nose as I stand up and head to the back door. "It's not your fault, but thank you. I appreciate it." No sarcasm this time. No anger or resentment. I mean it this time. "Do you wanna grab some food somewhere before I crash?"

"Oh, thank fuck! I'm glad you were thinkin' it too. I'd give my left nut for a decent meal right now."

We pile back into the Beast, and Devon starts it up. "Devon?"

He adjusts the rearview mirror to see me.

"I'm glad you decided to come along with me."

"You'll have plenty of time without me once we get back. Honestly, I'm not too eager to be on my own, either."

He backs out of the spot and pulls back onto the highway as I close my eyes, feeling the last of the warm sunlight splash over me.

Hour no idea of fifteen. It's dark as shit when I wake up, except for the occasional streetlight overhead. I wipe my eyes, clearing the crust from their corners, and blink a few times. Devon must be playing some music off my phone, or else I'm hallucinating John Denver's "Leaving on a Jet Plane." I'm about to sit up and ask Devon where we are when he sucks in a wracking breath and covers his mouth with one hand. His eyes flick up to the rearview, and I lie as still as humanly possible, snapping my eyes closed.

After a few seconds, I hear him take another heavy, wavering breath. He's clearly trying to hide them, but he's doing a poor job of it. He croaks out a few of the words to the song before his voice gives out. Snivels and sobs replace the lyrics.

Oh, boy, what the hell do I do now? Should I say something? I don't want him to feel embarrassed because then I'll feel terrible, and that'll just make everything worse. Should I just pretend to be asleep until the song ends? Maybe it'll pass. "Leaving on a Jet Plane" isn't that long.

As the thought crosses my mind, the last few chords strum out, and the car falls silent.

All right, cool. Now I just have to...

I crack one eye open as Devon pulls my phone out of the cupholder and taps the screen. The song starts up again, along with Devon's muffled weeping.

Oh. Okay. It's gonna be one of those evenings. Well, I can't just leave him like this.

"You doing okay, bud?"

Devon immediately stiffens up, sucking a nauseating combination of air and snot back up into his nose. "Did I... did I wake you?" His voice is a breathy, ragged mess.

How long has he been at this?

"No, you didn't. It sounds like you're having some trouble, is all." I sound remarkably calm for how panicked I feel. "Anything I can do?"

Devon tries to say something, but the words catch in his throat as a huge sob bursts out instead.

I have never seen Devon actually cry before. I've seen him right before or directly after, but never during. It's a heartbreaking sight I hope to never see again because I know the anguish behind sobs like that all too well.

I sit up and put my hands on his shoulders. "It's all right, my dude. You're all right."

"No, I'm not!" he bellows between fast, gasping breaths. "This whole th-th-thing is so... so fucked!"

"I know it is, but you're gonna get through it because you're a tough guy, right?" I squeeze his shoulders gently. I don't want to make him make any sudden movements while driving like this.

"I don't want to keep... keep... keep being tough. I'm s-s-s-sick of it. So fu-fucking sick of it."

"All right, bud, hold on." I lift the plastic bag we've been using as a trash bin out of the passenger seat and set it in the loft. I squeeze between the two seats as Devon looks back and forth between me and the road.

"Wh-what are you doing?"

"I'm coming up to sit with you."

"This is... is... is my issue, I ha-have to deal w-w-w-with it myself."

I pick up my phone and lower the volume so he won't keep riling himself up with the song.

"I know how you're feeling, bud. Probably better than most people, right?"

"Mhmm-mm." Devon nods, biting his lips together in a desperate effort to contain his sobs. As a streetlight passes overhead, I can see his whole face is red and damp.

"Have you been listening to that song on repeat?"

Devon nods again. His movements are frantic and jerky as his whole body shakes. I open the glove compartment and pull out a couple of tissues I stashed away back in Cali.

"Why we-we-were you hiding th-those?"

"I was saving them for jerking off with if we had to sleep in the car." I give him a cheeky smile, and he returns a small, momentary one before the weight of his burden crushes it beneath another wracking wail. I turn and sit with my back against the door, facing him.

"Talk to me, dude. Take a deep breath, and tell me what's got you so messed up. Okay?"

Devon nods, trying to keep his breath from jerking or jumping as he answers. "I was listening to some music on your phone to keep me occupied while you were sleeping, and this song came on, and my... my..." Another heaving breath washes over him, breaking into pitiful snivels.

"Easy, dude, easy. Breathe. Do you wanna pull over and take a minute?"

He shakes his head vigorously as if the very idea of stopping before we make it to the airport terrifies him. He gulps down another breath before continuing.

"My dad, he traveled a lot for work when I w-was little, and he'd... he'd always sing me this song when I'd g-get upset that he had to go away again." He takes one of the tissues off the center console and blows his nose. He balls up the used tissue and drops it into his lap. "I didn't know you had this song on your ph-ph-phone."

I used to love John Denver because of my dad, too, but he was more of a "Country Roads, Take Me Home," happy song John Denver fan.

"So, the song upset you?"

"Mm-m-mhmm." He takes another tissue, wiping his eyes this time. "I haven't listened to the song in a-a-a-ages, and I started singing along. It m-m-makes me think of him, and then I th-thi-think of him just lying there, all me-me-messed up." He starts to break down again, but I've got an idea now.

"You said singing the song makes you think of him, but instead of thinking about what's going on right now, how about we think about some good memories instead? Let's think of some better times. Okay?"

I restart the song and crank it to full blast on my phone, making sure to prop it up in the cupholder to amplify the sound.

"You ready?" I ask, but he shakes his head.

"I'm gonna sound b-b-bad."

"Dude, you hear me sing in the shower every day, and I sound *ass* bad. But I'll tell you what." I roll down the front windows, letting the cool night air rush into the car. The music is just audible enough to follow over the roar of the wind. "How's this?"

Devon shakes his head again.

"Sorry, I can't hear you over the wind!" I shout as I restart the song and start singing along.

Three words in, my voice cracks. I mean like *ugly* cracks, not the suave shit pop singers do. I start laughing, and I can see Devon smiling a little as he jumps in for the chorus with me. Two idiots screaming along to John Denver in the middle of God-knows where at Jesus-Christ-o'clock.

Devon's dad is gonna love hearing about this.

As we cross into New York, the first inklings of daylight lap at the horizon, diluting the pitch black of night into a softer morning blue. We lost quite a bit of time to some serious road work in the last bit of Ohio, so our fifteen-hour drive is now creeping into its seventeenth hour.

We decided to switch drivers a little ways into Pennsylvania, knowing it would be easier and faster for me to be the one driving when we arrive at JFK. Devon can just hop out, grab his suitcase from the trunk, and dash inside without having to switch places with me.

As we weave through cars on the Belt Parkway, silence has overtaken the Beast. But not an awkward silence, pleading to be filled with something, anything, no matter how deranged or stupid. No, the warm, contemplative silence that follows finishing a good movie or an amazing meal. No need to say anything because everyone there is already on the same page; no words needed.

As we pull off onto the special JFK stretch of private highway, I can't help but hesitate to break the delicate, amiable silence hanging between us.

"Which terminal are you leaving from?"

"Southwest."

I flick my eyes from the road to look at him. A shit-eating grin is plastered from ear to ear as the overtired giggles bubble up into laughter from both of us.

"That wasn't even funny!" I cry between fits of laughter so hard they make my stomach hurt a little.

"I beg to differ, old chap," Devon says in a terrible British accent. He tips an invisible hat to me and adjusts his monocle before telling me to drop His Esteemed Greatness off at terminal B.

The giggles and fits continue until we pull up at the departures drop-off. He hops out of the Beast and throws open the trunk, yanking out his suitcase and setting it on the curb. The trunk slams closed. I shift into drive, but Devon knocks on the passenger window before I can pull away. I roll the window down, and he leans in.

"Thanks for the ride, my dude. I know it wasn't the trip we planned, but I think it worked out all right."

"I think it was exactly what we needed," I tell him with a smile. "And make sure you text Riley once you're through security."

He slaps the window frame and points at me. "Right! Good man. I completely forgot." He steps away from the Beast and waves as I pull away, leaving me truly alone for the first time in what feels like ages. I have a full week to kill before I start work and no idea how I'm going to spend it.

FIFTEEN

Spending so much time in our house alone is strange. I'm sitting on the couch, drinking a beer, watching some TV, and I have to keep reminding myself Devon isn't home. After six days of having the house to myself, I thought I'd adjust, but I still catch myself pausing the TV on a particularly funny moment to show Devon, only to realize he's in Arizona, not his bedroom.

The days have been simultaneously instant and eternal. Each passing moment feels like a century, but it also feels like I just dropped Devon off at JFK two hours ago. I took the Beast in to get its steering pump fixed on Monday. Waiting in that dealership was hellishly long, especially since they only had the news going on the TVs. God, that was already four days ago. I start work tomorrow. Jared Paulsen, Bank Teller. It's going to be miserable, especially if my sense of time stays this out-of-whack.

I finish my beer and set the empty bottle on one end of the couch. I check my phone for any updates from Devon. Nothing.

Here's hoping no news is good news.

I toss it on the couch next to me and pause the TV. I've watched three seasons of *House* since I got back. It was my favorite show growing up, but the clever and cruel Dr. House trying to convince himself he's better off alone just doesn't hit the same in an empty home.

    I switch the input on the TV to my PlayStation with the remote and grab one of the controllers off the coffee table. In the momentary darkness of the inputs switching, I realize it's getting dark out because it's practically pitch black inside the apartment. The TV reconnects, filling the room with light again, casting away the dark. I scroll through my games: *Call of Duty*, *Destiny*, *Death Stranding*, and countless others. I aimlessly cursor between them before settling on *Destiny*, purely out of habit. The title screen loads, but I don't press X to start. It isn't the same without someone to cheer me on or tell me how bad I am. I set the controller back on the coffee table.

    I've played enough games in the dark.

    My legs swing up onto the couch as I tuck a hot pink, floral patterned pillow with "THUG LIFE" written on it under my head. I move the beer bottle to the floor, so I don't send it flying by accident. No need to spend my last day of freedom picking up glass. Not like I've done much else.

    I open my phone and peruse my contacts. Maybe someone'll be free and want to hang before I become a corporate drone. I send out a few texts but don't really expect to hear back. Everybody's either home with their families or too tired from their own jobs. Or both, I guess.

    My first days of actual adulthood. Spent in the dark. Alone. No more far-off places to explore, no more games to play or shows to watch. Nobody to hang out with. Settling into the mundane feels like sinking into a tar pit. I drop my phone on my chest and stare up at the ceiling. The dim light from the TV washes over me like an ocean wave. Is this what the rest of my life will be like? Bumming around on my off time until I go gray and die?

God, no wonder so many people are depressed. We spend our entire childhood looking forward to adulthood. We ask each other what we want to be and do, where we'll live and how big our houses will be. And then we get there. We work our jobs and live far apart in great, big houses filled with nothing and no one, and we peer backward over our shoulders to remember the past rather than face the grim, shrinking future.

I toss my phone on the coffee table and sit up. I need to do something, or else I'm gonna have an existential crisis. I pick my beer bottle up and head into the kitchen. Turning the light on makes me wince. I drop it in the recycling bin and look out the window. The Beast sits patiently in the driveway, waiting eagerly for somewhere to go.

I open the cabinets, looking for a snack or something to munch on for dinner, but the shelves are annoyingly bare.

I should've gone to the store today.

I flick the light off in the kitchen and head through the living room to my bedroom. The place is still a God-forsaken mess, now with the addition of the star map tube and my antique tea set. Still haven't unpacked my suitcase or satchel bag yet, either. I don't have any room for more dirty clothing. I sit on my bed, feeling the minutes drift into the irretrievable past.

I grab my satchel bag and pull my journal out. Haven't touched this since I got back, either. I leaf through the blank pages, feeling their thick, almost cottony grain. I've given up on trying to write something in it.

What's the point? It'll stay blank forever, a constant reminder of the life I missed out on. Am missing out on.

I stare at it, feeling myself sink deeper into the tar. How am I supposed to do this for the rest of my life?

All right. This is fucking stupid, and it's getting me nowhere. I need to do something, literally anything, to get my mind out of this fuckin' rut.

I set the journal aside, stand up, and stuff both arms into Mount Laundry. My hands find the small, plastic handles of my hamper. As I pull forward, the mountaintop caves in, and the white laundry basket comes free from the behemoth. The clothes inside have been compacted for months. I pull them out, one by one, and shake them vigorously to get the dust off and to reshape them into actual clothing. As I shake out the last pair of ancient underwear, I realize I have no clue if we still have any laundry detergent.

I lug the hamper down to the basement and find a half-full bottle of detergent on one of the lint-caked shelves. I dump in some soap, drop in the clothes, and set it to run. The machine thrums to life, and I feel the tar recede slightly. I head upstairs to refill the hamper. I don't care how long it takes; I need to get this shit done. I've put it off long enough.

Eight loads, by my count. Maybe eight and a half if I count the handful of pants I had to run through the dryer twice. Scooping the last of my clean clothes out of the dryer, I breathe a sigh of relief. I've worked up a good sweat hefting this shit back and forth. As I carry the hamper back up the stairs, I catch a glimpse of the deep blue, early morning sky through the kitchen window. I don't think the sun's up yet, though.

My sleep schedule is so fucked. I woke up at four in the afternoon today. I guess this is my opportunity to reset it.

I fold the laundry and put it in my dresser. It really is amazing how insurmountable Mount Laundry looked, and yet, with a little effort, it all fits snuggly in my dresser. I set the now-empty hamper back in the newly-cleaned corner. There's still plenty to do, but that's a start.

I unfurl my star map and hang it above the hamper since I can get to the wall now.

God, I am craving a cigarette. I know they're still in my bag, but I shouldn't have them. I just haven't gotten around to ditching them.

The cravings have gotten worse since I got home. With nothing to distract me like on the road, I can't get the bastards out of my head. I miss getting to take a little seven-minute break from life, feeling that nicotine rush spin out my head to someplace better. But that's it, isn't it? It's just in my head. It isn't real.

I go through my drawers, assembling the outfit I'll crawl into in a few hours before going to work. I take out a pink and black floral button-down, with rolled sleeves, of course, and a pair of tight black jeans. I drape them both over my desk chair and feel a little pang of sadness.

Did I waste my last few days of freedom? I mean, what's left to do? The sun's gonna be up any minute now, and I... I know just what to do.

I grab my journal and race outside.

Standing on the hood of the Beast, my fingertips just barely touch the edge of the roof. The leather cover of my journal tastes terrible, but I'm gonna need both hands for this maneuver. I would prefer not to land ass first on the driveway, or worse, back on the hood. Plus, the neighbors probably wouldn't like me screaming at five in the morning with a busted tail bone.

I rock my arms back and forth to get a little momentum going. I can feel the hood flexing slightly beneath my feet with each rock.

I got this.

I bend my knees as my arms swing down, then spring up, fully extending my legs and letting the momentum carry me up. My hands find the ledge. I pull up until I can hook my elbows over, then swing my leg up over the lip. I stand up and wipe nasty roof shit off my hands on my pants. I scan the Beast's hood for any dents or damage, but it looks fine to me. The old thing's really grown on me. It's a dumpster fire on wheels, but it got us home safe.

I climb to the apex of the roof and sit, setting my journal on my lap. Looking out over the trees and neighboring houses, I can see a few of the university buildings a little ways off, jutting into the sky as if reaching up to snatch at the clouds.

As the deep blue of early morning relents to warmer blues and yellows, I make myself comfortable and wait.

I've always been a night owl, just like my dad. We used to milk every minute out of our days together by staying up all night and watching the stars. It's funny how much I forgot while grieving. See, Amelia helped me remember how much I loved astronomy, but my dad was the one who taught me to love the sky.

That first apartment he moved into, the one he destroyed the vase in, was right next to the town's high school. So, we used to sneak out with our telescopes and lay in the football field, looking up at the stars. Then, when the sun would start to come up, we'd climb up into the stands and watch it rise over the building.

"As long as the sun comes up over that horizon, everything'll be okay, little man." He'd tell me that every time. And it always did, without fail. The next day came, and yesterday's problems slipped further and further away.

The first beams of light dance across the horizon, painting the base of the sky burnt umber, then vermillion, then orange. The lazy clouds and building tops ignite in beautiful pinks as the watercolor sky blends and brightens. As the minutes tick by, the sun breaks over the horizon, spilling warm light across the earth like paint. It's beautiful, and breathtaking, and humbling.

My phone buzzes in my pocket. I pull it out.

Dad's getting out today! the text from Devon reads. *He's gonna need a cane, but he'll be fine.*

Joy swells up in me, and I let rip a loud whoop at the horizon.

You were right, Daddio. It took me a while to figure it out, but you were. Everything will be okay.

I start typing out my response when another message comes through. A message from Amelia:

Are you free to talk today?

Something strange swirls inside me as I read it. Not the usual panic or fear I've come to expect, but something different. My fingers hover over the screen as I try to parse this new feeling.

I've waited for this for two weeks, and now? Am I ready for this? It feels like a lifetime ago since I stumbled down this street, lucky to be alive after the worst night of my life. All I've wanted to do since that night was talk to her. But now that moment's arrived, and I don't think it's what I want anymore. I need to remember how to be me for me again.

I tuck my phone back into my pocket. I can call Devon after work, but right now, I have to do something more important.

I open my journal and look over the first page with determination. I pull my pen from my pocket and uncap it.

No going back now.

The new day's light washes over me as the nib of my pen dances across the top of the first page:

This is for me, only me, and that is enough.

NOTES

1 Damasio, Antonio, Paola Antonelli, and Ricky Jackson. "Euthanasia Coaster (Julijonas Urbonas)." Design and Violence, April 23, 2014.

ACKNOWLEDGMENTS

An incredible thank you to my entire publishing team and to the amazing people who preordered my book, such as: Mary Jane Herwig, Cindy Mattioda, Kathleen Nelson Speer, Anna Gautrau, Michael Lee, Albert Rutecki, Kevin Clarke, Kimberly A. Korfel, Louisa Lacurci, Randy E. Imhoff, Kathy Boerema, Christopher Becker, Andra Lou Millerd, Xander Cavanagh, Jennifer Atkinson, Jodi Lang, Mike Williams, Christine Carey, Polly LeClaire, Nicole LeClaire, Donna Hill, Maverick Sciarrino, Kimberly Lum, Alexandra Wagner, Colleen Murphy, Frances R. Paul, Daniel Artuso, Laurie Dollner, Alex Howland, Dylan Stewart, Susie Bigelow, Maddie Wright, Steven Plotkin, Lois Goodin, Benjamin Haberman, Maya Deschenes, Sarah Lynch, Mathew Haigis, Mario Ramirez, Eric Koester, Bertha Krysztopik, Caroline Louise, Thomas Lee, Sarah Frankel, Jared Lucier, Lauren Dietzel, McKenzie Caldwell, Emily MacLean, Miranda Kent, Gary Krysztopik, Tia Harewood-Millington, Isabella Macallister, Erica A. Lang, Joy Grabow, Trenton Thomas, Kelly Slavin, Shaun Hayford, Paul Flanigan, Elizabeth Goodin, Danalisa Riccio, Alanna Bagdon, Elizabeth Rivard, Jeanne Wilson Stevens, Connor Imhoff, Scott Mathews, Thomas R. Kohl, Erik Mathews,

Nick Hoult, Ellen Anderson, Joan Calhoun Miller, Dr. Janis Lucky, David Krysztopik, and Stephanie Mathews.

None of this would've been possible without your generous support. Thank you all.

Made in United States
North Haven, CT
31 January 2022